OWN YOUR FUTURE

with REAL ESTATE

The Quick-Start Guide to Replacing Your Salary by Renting Out Single-Family Homes

ALIK LEVIN

CONTENTS

Dedicated to Inna, the love of my life

INTRODUCTION

Overview

Imagine you are over 40 years old and have been earning a six-figure salary for some time now. You own a home that is gaining good equity and have two decent cars (one leased). You have three kids, one of whom was just admitted to an in-state college. (Hint: That's $60K for just the tuition, but she informed you that she wants to move out to experience student life to the fullest, which is probably another $60K.) You have accumulated a healthy balance in your 401(k). You feel good about how you are handling your financial situation.

Let's narrow that down: You feel good about how you are handling your financial situation now. But then it hits you: You have two more kids to send to college, which is a couple of hundred thousand dollars more. You are getting older, and you face fierce competition in the workforce from young, hungry Millennials, automation, and an offshore workforce. What if the next industry swing makes your specialization obsolete? What if your 401(k), which is tied to the stock market, goes bust like it does from time to time? You think about the last financial crisis, where folks lost something like 40% of their 401(k) account value.

You wonder if you will be able to stay afloat, and, if so, for how long? If you lose your job, will anyone hire you with comparable pay now that you are past 40? And if not, what then? *The kids will be able to get the student loans, but what about me?* you ask yourself. *Will I be able to retire comfortably? Will I need to exist on Social Security that is barely solvent?*

You start chatting with your friends and co-workers about what they do to get ready for retirement. After a few chats at the water cooler, different approaches emerge: Some stick to the daily grind and don't pay attention to retirement; some invest heavily in stocks and try to beat the market; some opt for bonds for long-term gain; some hoard gold and silver in case the bubble busts, thinking they'll be able to pay for a loaf of bread with gold bullion; and some invest in real estate. Some opt for a little bit of everything, citing "diversification." You realize that folks are aware of the retirement challenges, and yet the majority are going down the beaten path of 401(k) retirement savings plans or stocks, which, in my view, are the same thing with different levels of control.

My 401(k) performance. Yuck!

Recently, I had lunch with a friend who defended the 401(k) model. The 401(k) model is based on tax-deferred contributions that gain compound interest, with the capital gains being tax free. (Note, however, that withdrawals from your 401(k) account become regular taxable income.) Employers also have the option of "matching" your contribution.

I questioned him on the calculations of past 401(k) performances, which heavily contradicted 401(k) future models. He scratched his head but was reluctant to agree with the calculations. Facts can be hard to swallow. I showed him my 401(k) performance as another example, which, when compared to main indexes, underperformed in both cases: When the indexes fell, my 401(k) fell faster. When the indexes grew, my 401(k) grew slower. "Oh," he said. "You need to control your 401(k)." I agreed and informed him that I had divested from the 401(k) program quite some time ago and had not contributed a penny since then. I wanted my money to work for me now, not potentially in the future. There are plenty of articles providing opinions on how the 401(k) program is failing its investors.

Often, 401(k) programs and compound interest are sold disingenuously, quoting Albert Einstein who said, "Compound interest is the eighth wonder of the world." Can you argue with a genius? You can't. (Hint: Actually, you can and you should, but many don't, so they follow the well-trodden 401(k) path.) Recently, I stumbled upon an article that revealed the rest of Einstein's quote, which had been omitted. It reads, "He who understands it [compound interest], earns it; he who doesn't pays it."[1] The same article then drives the last nail into the compound-interest model coffin: "Compounding only works when there is NO CHANCE of principal loss."[2] 401(k) investments are tied to stocks or other volatile financial instruments that are not backed by anything real; for example, gold. Therefore, can it lose principal? Sure it can, and it has, and it will continue to. Compound that!

I asked fellow future retirees about their thoughts on real estate investment. Some mentioned that they had invested in real estate; however, it turned out they were referring to their own home as the investment vehicle. That is still somewhat promising because a house is tangible and can't lose its 'principal' completely. Even if property values go down, a house won't evaporate like stocks can. Other folks challenged me back with statements such as, "Real estate? Like managing rentals? Wouldn't it be easier to invest in REITs?" (A Real Estate Investment Trust is another fancy financial instrument backed by nothing more than numbers on paper.) They went on to say, "The thought of dealing with pesky tenants gives me goose bumps! No rentals for me, oh no!"

What's an aspiring retiree to do?

1 Tyler Durden, "5 Financial Myths You Should Ignore," Zero Hedge, March 22, 2017, www.ZeroHedge.com/news/2017-03-22/5-financial-myths-you-should-ignore.
2 *Ibid.*

Try punching your own numbers to see how much your own net worth could go up with rental properties:

ENTER TRANSACTION DETAILS HERE				
Purchase Price	$ 500000	Homeowners Insurance	$ 500	
Down Payment	$ 100000	Yearly Taxes	$ 4000	
Loan Interest Rate	4.2 %	Monthly expenses/ Maintenance fees	$ 100	
Loan Term in Years	30			
Monthly Rental	$ 2300			
Rent Increase Yearly	4.0 %			
Inflation (for ins, taxes, expenses)	2 %	Your Gross Income (for tax calculation)	$ 100000	
Property Value Growth (real estate appreciation)	5.4 %			

RESULTS					
Loan Amount	$ 400000		Monthly Payment	$ 1956	

INCOME	Year 1	Year 2	Year 3	Year 4	Year 5
Rental Income	27600	28704	29852	31046	32288
EXPENSES					
Insurance	500	510	520	530	541
Taxes	4000	4080	4161	4244	4329
Monthly Expenses/Fees	1200	1224	1248	1273	1298
Total Payments	23472	23472	23472	23472	23472
Total Expenses	29172	29286	29401	29519	29640
CASH FLOW					
Cash Flow	-1572	-582	451	1527	2648
TAX DEDUCTION					
Interest Expense	16800	16548	16296	16128	15960
+ Depreciation*	16363	16363	16363	16363	16363
+ Ins, Tax, other expenses	5700	5814	5929	6047	6168
- Rental Income	27600	28704	29852	31046	32288
Total Tax Deduction	11263	10021	8736	7492	6203
TAX SAVED**	3491	3106	2708	2322	1922
NET WORTH					
After Tax Cash Flow	1919	2524	3159	3849	4570
Principal Paid (est)	6672	6924	7176	7344	7512
Property Value	527000	555458	585452	617067	650388
Yearly addition to Net Worth	35591	37906	40329	42808	45403

www.goodmortgage.com/Calculators/Investment_Property.html

Then I read *Rich Dad Poor Dad* by Robert Kiyosaki, *The Millionaire Next Door* by Thomas J. Stanley, and *Sell or Be Sold* by Grant Cardone. Reading these books opened my eyes to the world and guided me down the investment path that I had been searching for. Since then, I have read many more books on topics involving rental property investments. It has cost me money and time—a lot of it—but it was worth it. I took an initial step and purchased my first rental property, followed by another, and then a few more. I haven't looked back since.

I initially wrote this book for myself and am now gladly sharing it with you. It documents my path toward financial freedom in retirement, and it puts me on notice by publicly stating that I am relentless in getting what I want when I retire, which I plan to do by the age of 50. And I want a lot by then. I don't plan on retiring poor, which, by the way, is another way the 401(k) model fails its investors: It assumes that, when you retire, your taxes will be lower because you won't earn as much as you do today. Thus, when you pull funds from your 401(k), you will be taxed less than you would have been during your working years. What a bunch of nonsense. Here's a news flash: I don't plan on retiring poor! I asked myself, Why should I give Wall Street my money to play Russian roulette with, while they point the gun my way, until I am 65?

I spent countless hours online, purchased multiple books and audiobooks, and paid hundreds of dollars to consultants and experts only to realize that I needed to hire more. It is hard to estimate how much it cost me to pull this book together, but it is well worth the value. I can safely estimate the value in thousands of dollars in cash flow, and even more in net worth. This is far more valuable than realized income because wealth isn't taxed... yet.

Since implementing what I cover in this book, my net worth has grown by tens of thousands of dollars annually. Lenders love net worth, especially when they are asked to provide loans for other investment properties. Exactly how much do they love it?

As of this writing, my outstanding debt secured by realty is over $2,000,000. That may sound counterintuitive. How can such a large debt be a sign of financial success? Sounds fair, but consider this: In every book that I have read by Robert Kiyosaki (I think I am on his fifth), he points out that your financial statements are your report cards to your lender. If the lender likes your financial statements (your real-life report cards),

STOCKS vs. RENT

$100K invested in stocks over five years would gain $40K.

$100K invested in rental properties over the same five years will increase in net worth/equity by over $200K.

"The average American millionaire realizes significantly less than 10 percent of his net worth in annual income. In spite of having considerable wealth and substantial annual increases in wealth (in unrealized form), the typical American millionaire may personally be cash poor."

Thomas J. Stanley
The Millionaire Next Door

he will lend you money. I guess my lender likes my report card (my financial statements) a lot since he is willing to lend me $2,000,000. Here is another measure of success I use: In my first year of implementing the techniques outlined in this book, my annualized gross income from real estate was comparable to what I earned from my day job. To put that into perspective, I have over 20 years' tenure in the software industry in the greater Seattle area. That should give you a good idea of my current compensation level.

Remember, though, that it took me 20 years to financially get where I am today with my day job. Compare that to what I achieved in one year by following the guidance I received from countless sources. The very guidance that I have carefully curated and placed in this book.

Let's do some more math, shall we?

Imagine you have $100K to spare for an investment of your choosing. You have two options:

1. Investing in stocks.
2. Purchasing rental property over a 5-year period.

Let's break it down:

OPTION 1 – INVESTING IN STOCKS. For simplicity's sake, let's assume you invest in a major S&P 500 Index, which usually outperforms most fund management firms. It's assumed that, over a long period, stock performance is 8% on average. We assume that no principal loss occurs for the next five years (sterile lab conditions). Here is the resulting investment outcome:

- ▶ End of Year 1 - $100K * 8% = $108K – 15% capital gains tax, balance = $106.8K
- ▶ End of Year 2 - $106.8K * 8% = $ 115.344K – 15% capital gains tax, balance = $ 114.1K
- ▶ End of Year 3 - $ 114.1K * 8% = $ 123.2K – 15% capital gains tax, balance = $ 121.8K
- ▶ End of Year 4 - $ 121.8K * 8% = $ 131.6K – 15% capital gains tax, balance = $ 130.1K
- ▶ End of Year 5 - $ 130.1K * 8% = $ 140.5K – 15% capital gains tax, balance = $ 138.9K

Congrats! Your $100K and compounding earned you almost $40K over five years, and your net worth is that much higher! Einstein would be proud. The harsh reality, though, is that some five-year periods earn less than 8%, some earn more, and some are entirely in the red. Therefore, a lot depends on when you start to invest and when you pull your money out of the Wall Street Russian roulette game.

OPTION 2 – INVESTING IN RENTAL PROPERTY. Typically, $100K gets you a property worth $500K when you finance it through a lender with a 20% down payment. This is the industry standard, but scenarios may vary. Depending on geographic location, charging $2,300/ month for rent is realistic for a 3- or 4-bedroom house. Property values appreciate on average 5.4% nationally. In hot housing markets, the average appreciation can be as high as 19%. In fact, one of my properties recently appreciated 16% annually, so I sold it for a 25% cash-on-cash return on investment (ROI). Now stock market that!

Rent typically appreciates at 4% annually, but let's assume for simplicity that monthly liabilities break even and that there is zero cash flow monthly. Loans are usually structured so that, in the beginning, you pay back two-thirds in interest payments and one-third of your principal. Here is the breakdown:

- End of Year 1 - $500K * 5.4% appreciation = $527K, Liability $394K
- End of Year 2 - $527K * 5.4% appreciation = $555.5K, Liability $388K
- End of Year 3 - $555.5K * 5.4% appreciation = $585.5K, Liability $382K
- End of Year 4 - $585.5K * 5.4% appreciation = $617.1K, Liability $376K
- End of Year 5 - $617K * 5.4% appreciation = $650.4K, Liability $370K

By the end of Year 5, your net worth is calculated as follows:

$650.4K property value

less $370.0K remaining mortgage balance

$280.4K in net worth increase

Compound that!

Now let's assume you sell the property and are taxed at the 15% capital gains tax bracket, resulting in a profit of $240K (less 8% commissions and excise tax). This leaves you with a total close to $200K. Very nice, eh?

But why even pay that $80K in capital gains and excise tax and commissions? Alternatively, you can take another loan based on the equity in the property accumulated over five years and purchase another property or two! With $280K in equity, you could get yourself two more rental houses, each worth $500K or more.

It gets better.

The IRS allows you to deduct approximately *one-27.5th* of your original property cost annually as a legitimate deduction (phantom expense). This is because the IRS considers that the property loses its total value in 27.5 years. For that property, it is $91K of legitimate deductions in property depreciation over a five-year period that nicely offsets the capital gains in case you sell it. It also potentially offsets most, if not all, rent gains over that period. In simple terms, you pay no tax whatsoever, and the IRS knows it and recognizes it! Compare that to the 15% capital gains tax on stocks that you pay regardless of whether or not you sell the stocks (precision omitted for simplicity)!

So what would it be? **Option 1 with $40K hard cash in hand** *or* **Option 2 with three rental properties** *or* **$200K hard cash in hand**? Remember, it all started with a $100K investment in both cases.

In the following chapters, I cover key concepts, strategies, guidelines, and how-to's that I've learned over the years, and I'm excited to share them with you! This book will give you the foundation you need to start feeling comfortable investing in single-family rental homes.

Read on, but please remember:

- ▶ **I am not a tax professional.**
- ▶ **I am not a real estate professional.**
- ▶ **I am not an accredited business consultant.**
- ▶ **I am not a bookkeeper.**
- ▶ **I am not an attorney.**
- ▶ **I am not an incorporation specialist.**
- ▶ **I am not anything or anyone that requires a license for any of the professional fields discussed in this book.**

I document my personal experience backed by authoritative references that I have learned on my journey toward financial freedom.

By reading this book, you agree to keep me, my family, my associates, and my companies out of any liability that you may encounter. This book is my personal story that I am sharing with you. You can choose to use my story for guidance or not. Investment is a risk, and you should fully realize that and make your own choices. Here is another, dry version of the same:

This book contains general legal and/or tax information. It is not advice and should not be treated as such.

Risk

One question I'm consistently asked when sharing my approach to real estate investment is, "What about the risk? Your book makes it sound too easy, and the picture too rosy. Remember what happened in 2008?"

I get it: Investing is risky. In fact, I mention risk in the beginning of my book. Keep in mind that this book represents **my** story. It's about how I took the plunge and created a clear, systemic approach so that I could see the full terrain, and anticipate risk. With this approach, I could respond effectively to risk, and better yet, avoid risk altogether.

This book is not about how risk-free real estate investing is. This book is about how to use a systematic approach to create clarity so that you can make effective real estate investments. Real estate, like any other investment, has its risks. Similarly, relying solely on a day job for financial security carries its own risks.

Q. What if you have tenants from hell?

A. What if you had a manager, neighbor, or customer from hell? To address this question specifically, my book contains a chapter on how to target property niches that attract desired tenants, and how to identify and mitigate potential red flags within legal boundaries.

Q. What if the market tumbles, like it did in 2008?

A. What if you get fired from your job? Just like they did in 2008, stock values may plummet, but properties remain properties, and renters typically don't flee the very next day. My book further addresses this question. It describes how to evaluate property for cash flow and appreciation so that you can grow equity for situations like these, where, should you need to reduce your rent, you can cash in or have a financial cushion in place. The best approach is to target areas where there is solid population growth and ensuring that growth is meaningful.

Q. What if a tenant calls you at night stating that his toilet is clogged?

A. This question is more about tenant vs. landlord responsibilities and how to manage tenant expectations, and less about clogged toilets. My book contains a chapter that outlines each party's responsibilities. In this example, the landlord is not responsible for the tenant's clogged toilet.

Q. My accountant told me that, even when operating under a limited liability company (LLC), I am still personally liable in lawsuits involving my rental property.

A. Fire your accountant. Accountants have no business advising you on legal matters. Neither do I, for that matter, and I have a disclaimer in this book stating this fact, so feel free to fire me too. The chapter in this book about legal matters describes legal structures that may protect you personally from lawsuits—internal and external. As a bonus, after you fire your accountant, you may want to read the chapter on Tax Strategy, which talks about... well... tax strategy. It describes how to take advantage of the plethora of tax benefits involving real estate. Your accountant probably won't give you this information, as withholding it keeps his life simple during tax season.

The bottom line is that risk is better mitigated when identified up front vs. dealing with a mess after the fact. And this is exactly what this book is about—getting clarity on key aspects by using the Real Estate Investment Framework. I'll go into more detail on this topic in a bit, but using the Investment Framework will help you understand what to focus your attention on, risk-wise, and how to address or mitigate those risks. At the very least, it will help you learn the lingua franca so that, when hiring a professional, you can maintain a meaningful conversation, and even challenge their professional opinion where needed.

Risk, in my opinion, is when someone else controls my life or controls my finances. Having a 401(k) retirement plan is a risk because it is tied to a volatile market. Even worse, my hard-earned money is locked away for decades, being left to rot without my ability to control it. In the last downturn, people lost roughly 40% of the value in their "savings" programs. (I cannot bring myself to call it "savings" without quotes.)

Pension plans are also risky. States and local authorities have mismanaged pensions so badly that, nationally, liabilities overshadow assets in pensions programs by trillions of dollars (that is a lot of zeros: 1,000,000,000,000). But now that they have run out of money, pension benefits are being cut, even though people paid into these pensions their whole working lives.

Social Security is a risk. It's a Ponzi scheme where your money is taken from you now—whether you like it or not—and then spent by the government who gets into trillions of dollars of debt (there's those zeros again) while promising to pay you back when you are 65. Or 67. The age keeps going up. It's the mother of all risks, isn't it? And you talk about clogged toilets?

Stock markets are a risk. Tesla, Snapchat, Netflix, and other sexy and popular stocks are growing like crazy, but these companies show nothing in net operating income—and they are burning through investors' cash or depend on government subsidies. That's risk. Fund managers who make money on commissions, regardless of whether or not you make a profit—that's risk.

Day jobs are a risk. Robots and automation, getting older and less competitive vs. young and hungry, and wild swings in market needs are a daily reality. I have seen plenty of talented people being handed pink slips, in both stable and unstable times.

Risk is when someone else tells you how you should manage your hard-earned money. In this book, I share my story of how I managed my money by pulling it all from the stock market and "savings" programs and getting into more than $2,000,000 debt (isn't that an achievement by itself?) secured by cash flow and appreciating real estate properties. That's the risk I am willing to take, together with my friendly lender.

Clogged toilets aren't a risk. Property values that go down aren't a risk, abrasive tenants aren't a risk.

Wealthy people invest in real estate. I have researched enough on how wealthy people made it to the top. Tim Ferris interviewed

Arnold Schwarzenegger in his book, *Tools of Titans*, and, amongst other things, this is what Schwarzenegger had to say:

"Buildings that I would buy for $500K within the year were $800K, and I put only maybe $100K down, so you made 300% on your money[...] I became a millionaire from my real estate[...] before [I did] in show business."

How cool is that? Good for you, Arnie! If he could do it, then a software engineer like myself could do it too, and maybe even better, eh?

Risk isn't the issue for me. I want to break through the glass ceiling and be financially secure by the time I turn 50 and work only if I want to, not because I need to. With that goal in mind, real estate investing looks to me like the least risky path forward. My lender shares over $2,000,000 in risk with me, and these guys know a thing or two about risk, eh? I'm happy to partner with them and share the risk.

My final thought on risk: Read the book *Boss Life* by Paul Downs. It's a "Forbes Best Business Book of the Year, 2015." I listened to it as an audiobook during my morning runs. The key message I took from this book is that, if this guy can victoriously "survive his own small business," then I can survive creating passive income from rental properties. It motivated me to pursue the path to becoming an entrepreneur.

Motivation isn't sustainable by itself and needs to be constantly fed. To motivate myself in an ongoing manner, I chain read books on relevant topics. Well, I listen to them during my morning runs using the Audible app on my iPhone. In fact, I have a whole chapter in this book called "Continuing Education" where I talk about how I educate myself continuously. Back to motivation though. To keep my motivation high, I apply a positive affirmation technique every morning when I finish my 4.6-mile run.

Multiple books mention this technique, but two books are most prominent. One is the timeless classic by Napoleon Hill called *Think and Grow Rich*, and the other is by Scott Adams (the Dilbert guy) called *How to Fail at Almost Everything and Still Win Big*.

Every morning when I finish my 4.6-mile run, I proclaim my risk-combating positive affirmation out loud: "I, Alik Levin, am a very successful real estate entrepreneur with X million dollars in assets by the age of 50 and a Y dollars increase in net worth this summer."

Your X and Y may vary.

How to Use This Book

This book is structured around an approach I call the *Real Estate Investment Framework*, which is discussed in more depth in the next section. To put it simply, the Real Estate Investment Framework captures all the key aspects of managing rental properties at a glance and offers a balcony view or roadmap of the Real Estate Investment "terrain." Using this map makes it easier to see where you are right now and where you want to go, and it helps you chart a path forward between these two points. Each chapter goes deeper into each part of the Real Estate Investment Framework (e.g. target niche, financing, marketing, etc.) and contains the following sub-sections:

OVERVIEW. This section describes why you should care about a particular part of the Investment Framework. For example, the "Overview" section within Target Niche outlines examples of ways to make money by investing in real estate. It then describes how to narrow down on a strategy that resonates with you, so you can place laser-sharp focus on it without distractions and nail it.

DESIGN. This section helps you visualize the key components and their relationships. For example, the "Design" section within Marketing illustrates the tenant-screening process to help you identify a friction-free, ideal tenant within legal boundaries.

STRATEGY. This section outlines what you need to optimize around. For example, the "Strategy" section within Financing describes how to obtain financing that makes the numbers work for you vs. the other way around.

CONCEPTS. This section defines the industry jargon and "geek speak" for each part of the Real Estate Investment Framework. For example, the "Concepts" section within Property Management defines the concepts of "repairs and maintenance" and "property improvements," and it explains the difference between the two. There are huge differences when it comes to tax deductions and, ultimately, how your bottom line is impacted.

GUIDELINES. This section lays out the do's and don'ts. For example, in the "Guidelines" section within Legal Entity Structure , we discuss when it is reasonable to set up a Limited Liability Company (LLC) or a layered LLC, and when to consider not setting one up at all.

HOW-TO'S. This section provides step-by-step instructions. While the "Guidelines" sections discuss the do's or don'ts, the "How-To's" sections explain a task or process by breaking down the individual steps. For example, the "How-To's" section within Bookkeeping provides step-by-step procedures on how to set up and use a Property Depreciation Account in QuickBooks Online (or QBO in geek speak).

Additional sub-sections include "Scenarios" and "Solutions." This is similar to a case study where a scenario is presented, followed by a roadmap on how to solve the scenario using the above attributes (Design, Strategy, Concepts, Guidelines, and How-To's). In addition, multiple resources are offered at the end—for example, calculators, affiliated third parties, and references.

Now that you understand how to use this book, let's take a balcony view of the real estate investment terrain and briefly cover each of the main areas that make up the Real Estate Investment Framework.

The Real Estate Investment Framework

This section lays out the fundamentals of the approach outlined in this book, which I've been calling the Real Estate Investment Framework. This is the heart of it—the secret sauce. The Real Estate Investment Framework is made up of nine components that have a major impact on the overall bottom line. These include: target niche, financing, marketing, property management, legal entity structure, bookkeeping, tax strategy, continuing education, and networking. Focusing on only a few and neglecting others will surely open the door for undesired issues to arise which could easily be avoided upfront.

For example, if you found your perfect target niche, such as single-family home rentals (which is the focus of this book), and you found a way to narrow down how to manage your books, you may find that financing is a major stumbling block. You may also find that it manifests at the most inconvenient time, causing the whole invest-ment to unravel. Even if you started great—and your tenants enjoy the property, keep it clean, and pay on time—if you haven't addressed the tax strategy early on, you may find that your tax burden isn't what you had hoped for, and most of your hard-earned money ends up with Uncle Sam at the end of the tax season, when it's too late. The Real Estate Investment Framework helps reduce risks such as these and many others. It lays out the full picture at a glance and allows you to tackle each part early on and face relevant challenges prepared (versus frantically reacting in the heat of the battle).

The table on the following pages outlines each aspect of the Real Estate Investment Framework and why you should care about it. Familiarize yourself with the framework; the rest of the book is tightly coupled to it and is based on the concepts described in it.

Aspect	Why You Should Care
Target Niche	**Objective** ▶ To narrow down a profitable niche **Risks** ▶ Ineffectiveness in making profits due to a lack of focus ▶ Frustration and abandonment due to a lack of results or losses **Benefits** ▶ Expertise growth ▶ Exponential results in building wealth and net worth ▶ Investing becomes enjoyable
Financing	**Objective** ▶ Secure funds at preferable terms **Risks** ▶ The loss of an investment deal due to a lack of funds ▶ Negative cash flow due to less than optimal terms **Benefits** ▶ Securing a great deal ▶ Friction-free financing
Marketing	**Objective** ▶ Target and lease to highly qualified tenants **Risks** ▶ Losses due to the tenant being late on payments ▶ Losses on property value or cash flow due to tenant's negligence **Benefits** ▶ Property kept in top shape and ready to sell or rent instantly ▶ Uninterrupted cash flow
Property Management	**Objective** ▶ Keep property in top shape **Risks** ▶ Losses on property value due to tenant's negligence or misunderstanding of duties **Benefits** ▶ Property kept in top shape and ready to sell or rent instantly

Aspect	Why You Should Care
Legal Entity Structure	**Objectives** ▸ Protect personal assets ▸ Reduce tax liability **Risks** ▸ Personal assets may be exposed to law suits ▸ Higher tax liabilities **Benefits** ▸ Personal assets protected against law suits ▸ Business tax deductions
Bookkeeping	**Objectives** ▸ Reduce tax liability ▸ Reduce the time wasted on administrative tasks **Risks** ▸ Time waste ▸ Higher tax liability due to inaccuracy of records **Benefits** ▸ Keep more time to yourself ▸ Keep more money to yourself
Tax Strategy	**Objectives** ▸ Reduce tax liability short term ▸ Reduce tax liability long term **Risks** ▸ Higher tax liability now ▸ Higher tax liability later **Benefit** ▸ Keep more money to yourself
Continuing Education	**Objective** ▸ Improve business growth by communicating effectively **Risks** ▸ Being bamboozled ▸ Getting stuck due to ineffective communications **Benefits** ▸ Improved analysis of potential deals ▸ Growing business into new areas
Networking	**Objective** ▸ Improve effectiveness via scale out **Risk** ▸ Slow or no growth **Benefit** ▸ Faster growth via formal or thought partnerships

CHAPTER 1

Target Niche

Overview

How do you narrow down a profitable niche? For example, the software engineering vertical is highly profitable. On the other hand, IT security, software performance, and software architecture are all narrow yet hugely profitable niches. The same is true with real estate. Flipping houses; wholesaling; becoming a real estate agent; buying and holding; and investing in multifamily, single family, commercial property, and land are just a few niches.

That said, there are a few things at play, the most important of which are market condition, your financial strength, and your short- and long-term goals. I have zeroed in on Class B/C single-family homes (SFRs, as in Single-Family Residences) with large lots. Class B, from a location perspective, means homes in a desired location, and Class C, from an age perspective, means older homes. Older homes may sell at a lower price. They are relatively easy to spruce up without incurring carrying costs. Buying older homes in a desired location ensures I can quickly find qualified renters without keeping the property empty—thus avoiding carrying costs, such as bills and a mortgage. What usually helps is that the lender starts charging monthly mortgage payments after the first full month; meaning, if the home was purchased, closed, and financed on March 8th, then the first mortgage payment is due on May 1st. On top of that, lenders allow a 15-day grace period, so that gives you about two months to spruce up the home and find a qualified renter before making your first payment to the lender.

Larger lots usually hold the potential of *forced appreciation* (explained on page 4). This can be achieved through major remodeling or by parceling (subdividing) the large lot into smaller lots and building additional homes (either for sale or renting out). Single-family homes normally appreciate faster vs. multifamily. The bottom line: My ideal investment deal looks like the following:

- ▸ **An older, single-family home that requires some work (sweat equity).**
- ▸ **Sold under market price.**
- ▸ **Large lot.**
- ▸ **Desired location.**

Yours may look differently depending on where you are now and where you want to be, and how fast.

Design

Consider the following diagram. You, as the investor, are in the center surrounded by a multitude of potential real estate investment niches. When getting started, it's better to focus on only a few—or even just one. In the case below, we're looking at the single-family rental homes niche (the two circles in the box):

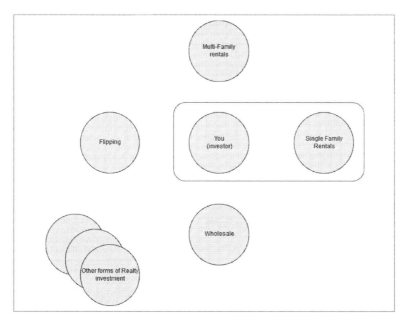

- ▶ **You** (**investor**). This is you, and you are surrounded by many choices of how to invest in real estate.
- ▶ **Multi-family rentals.** These are multi-family units (e.g. condos, duplexes, triplexes) that usually optimize around cash flow. They are not the focus of this book.
- ▶ **Single-family rentals.** These are single-family homes that usually optimize around appreciation—this book's focus.
- ▶ **Wholesale.** A real estate wholesaler puts a distressed home under contract with the intent to assign that contract to another buyer (usually an investor). This is something I have never considered and probably never will.
- ▶ **Other forms of realty investment not covered in this book.**

Strategy

The key objective in determining your target niche is to focus on the niche that best fits your style and meets your goals and desires. Consider the following desires and conditions:

1. **Long-term, tax-free wealth creation.** Wealth is not taxable. Realized income as in cash flow is taxable. When property appreciates, its worth or value grows, yet this value gain isn't taxed until it's sold.

2. **Faster appreciation.** I don't need cash now, as I have it from my day job. I'd rather see my property grow in value tax free, and the faster the better.

3. **Higher-income prospective tenants.** I'd like to deal with established tenants who are financially stable and prefer to rent from me longer to avoid disruptions in cash flow. This will help me reduce the turnover friction and overhead expenses related to vacancy and the move-in/move-out of tenants.

4. **Independence from HOAs.** An HOA, or homeowners association, can be a big constraint. Not only can an HOA decide to raise monthly fees (and if you are in the minority, you will need to pay), but also any changes you want to make to the property must be approved by the HOA. Quite an impediment for an investor in my book (or rather in *my* book), especially when it comes to forced appreciation—major renovations.

5. **Potential for forced appreciation.** Forced appreciation is when a change or addition to the property increases the property's value faster than usual appreciation. Some examples include: kitchen remodeling (for that, no one needs HOA's approval), better landscaping (HOA may well get in the way), or adding additional rooms that would require structural changes (forget about it if an HOA is at play).

Given the above desires and conditions, my best bet would be focusing on single-family homes as rentals. Usually, an HOA isn't at play with SFRs (single-family residences), but not always. SFRs usually appreciate faster than multi-family homes, and SFRs are usually sought after by established families that are financially stable who seek to settle for longer periods of time, as they wouldn't want their kids to move from school to school often. And they are my ideal tenants.

Concepts

▸ **Appreciation.** Appreciation is growth in the value of the property. For example, let's say you purchased a home for $100K. Next year, the value of the home is $109K (based on Redfin.com or Zillow.com or your county's assessor or professional appraiser). In this case, your home value appreciated by 9%.

▸ **Buy and hold.** Buy and hold is an investment strategy where a property is purchased and then held for a long period, thus the terms "buy" and "hold." The strategy serves to increase the home's equity and, as a result, increase the investor's net worth. The equity then can be used in multiple ways. For example, taking out a cash loan based on the increased equity and then purchasing additional investment property. Consider a property purchased originally for $100K with an annual appreciation of 6% annually over five years. We're talking about close to $35K equity growth in total. Taking out a cash loan for $35K may finance another property worth $175K. (Usually you need 20% down to purchase a house with bank financing, $35K*5=$175K.) Holding a $100K house for five years buys you another one worth $175K. Rinse and repeat. The "hold" part is important. As they say, "refi 'till you die." (I heard this on the Kathy Fettke podcast. Subscribe, I highly recommend it.) In other words, once purchased, never sell. When operating a rental property, one of the big benefits is claiming the depreciation deduction—a phantom expense that reduces tax liability. It's really magic and all legitimate. The magic turns into tragedy when you sell it; this is when the axe called the "depreciation recapture tax" is dropped. Long story short (I'll go into this in more detail in the following sections): Investors should hold their properties forever to avoid this depreciation recapture tax—or sell them through a 1031 exchange to defer taxes forever and then apply additional strategies down the line to legally avoid taxes altogether (which I haven't yet tried, but this topic is outside of the scope of this book). This is called an exit plan. I am yet to be anywhere close to the exit, but planning for it upfront is part of the grand design.

▸ **Cash flow.** Cash flow is about the monthly flow of cash that comes from rent paid by the tenant less expenses and liabilities, such as mortgage payments, insurance, and taxes. In the case of a long-term strategy, such as buy and hold, it's okay to just break even; meaning, no cash flow at all. Negative cash flow, when expenses and liabilities overshadow monthly rent, is usually a sign that something is broken with the numbers and deserves closer attention and fixing.

▸ **Equity.** Equity is the property's value minus any liabilities. For example, if the house is currently worth $100K and you owe the lender $55K, then the house's equity is $45K ($100K-$55K). Equity allows you to purchase more investment properties (good debt) or to cash in for consumer spending (bad debt, really bad). Yes, there is good and bad debt.

▸ **Flipping.** Flipping houses is a technique of getting quick cash. Buy an undesired, run-down property, spruce it up (causing forced appreciation), and then sell it at a higher price. This strategy is usually not suitable for beginners for a few reasons: 1) It's riskier, 2) It's harder to get financing, and 3) It exposes you to higher taxation, as it's not considered passive income.

▸ **Forced appreciation.** Forced appreciation is the technique of adding value to the property by improving the property significantly. For example, this includes kitchen remodeling, master suite remodeling, or all-over "up" remodeling. Forced appreciation allows you to charge higher rent. And because the property is usually appraised higher, it allows you to take out a higher cash loan to purchase more investment properties. Finally, when it's time to sell, it allows you to sell the house at a premium price.

▸ **Homeowners association (HOA).** An HOA is a group of

homeowners, usually the residents of a neighborhood or a multi-family building, who drive and enforce neighborhood rules, such as how tall the grass should be and how often you should mow it. It also collects HOA fees that may rise dramatically should the HOA decide to repair the roof or install AC in the building. If you are in the minority and outvoted, you are required to pay the increase.

▸ **Multi-family property.** Multi-family properties are usually properties other than single-family homes. There is something shared in a multi-family property. For example, it could be a shared wall, like it is in a duplex, or the whole roof that runs over an apartment complex.

▸ **Net worth.** Your net worth is your worth after you subtract all your liabilities from all your assets. Examples of assets can be cash, positive bank account balances, your car's value (if you own it outright), and your property's value. (Obviously, there are many other assets you should take into account, but these are a few examples.) On the other hand, liability is what you owe to creditors, such as credit card balances, mortgages, student loans, car loans, etc. For example, if the sum of your assets is worth $100K and the sum of your liabilities is $40K, your net worth is $60K.

▸ **Property classes.** It's possible to classify properties into classes. What I understand is that the classification system is mainly about the age of the property and the desirability of its location. For example, a Class A property is new and in a desired location, a Class B property is less than new and in a somewhat desired location, and a Class C property is... well, you get the point. Since one of the rules of thumb is that the investment rental property should be within a 30-minute drive of where you live, make sure to factor this into your classification. Set your own standards and factor in external attributes to assign scores to the properties. Mine are the age of the property (the older the property, the lower the purchase price will be, but the cost of getting it market ready may also go up), and the second factor is location (mainly, how close it is to job hubs and the ratings of schools in the neighborhood). I also have a third factor and that's the property's lot size. Your scoring attributes could be different than mine, but classifying properties is a good idea. New properties on small lots close to great schools may cash flow nicely, while older ones on larger lots may appreciate faster. Optimize your property classes around your short- and long-term goals.

▶ **Single-family property or single-family residence (SFR).** This is a property that can host only one family as opposed to multi-family properties.

▶ **Sweat equity.** Sweat equity is usually associated with a run-down property that is offered at a substantial discount (and below market price) but requires a lot of work. Sweat equity is about putting your personal effort into making the property livable and attractive to a potential renter. You invest your sweat, and you get equity in the form of property value in return. For example, if the property is offered at a $20K discount vs. market value, you can make it livable by investing your own time (and at near zero cost if you are a handyman). Or you could hire a handyman to do the work for $5K, which may result in a potential $15K savings. This is usually what professional flippers do at scale, but you could definitely do it yourself if the investment is something you are willing to undertake. With one of our properties, my wife and I painted the whole thing end to end—from the walls to the running boards. It took us a few days, but we saved thousands of dollars on labor and materials vs. what it would have cost had we outsourced it.

Guidelines

▶ **Master one narrow niche at a time.** When you get started, pick one niche and master it first; don't spread yourself thin. Focus on one thing at a time. Once mastered, you can continue doing it, expand to a new niche, or completely move over to something new if the current niche proves to be something you don't enjoy.

▶ **Target properties within a 30-minute drive.** You want to be able to visit your property with no lead time—for any number of reasons. It doesn't happen often, but when you do need to go to one of your properties, it shouldn't be a major disruption to your life. And when you travel there, make sure to record miles and the purpose of the trip so you can claim it as a deduction when filing taxes. When the property is within a 30-minute drive, it's non-disruptive. But over the year, these trips add up and turn into a nice tax deduction.

▶ **Use online resources to find target properties.** Zillow.com and Redfin.com are excellent online resources to conduct initial research. Among the insights these websites provide are market temperature (cold means buyers' market, hot is a sellers' market), a list of active and sold properties and their prices, how long the property took to sell, what it took to sell it (for example, multiple price cuts or going into a pending state after a few days), schools ratings, crime rates, rent estimates, future property value appreciation, property taxes, and mortgage estimates for monthly payments. You can set filters to narrow down to very specific criteria and even set alerts to notify you if a property within your criteria becomes available and listed on the market. The websites offer mobile apps, so the alerts can be delivered to you when you're on the go, and when it happens, you can use the same mobile phone to call your agent and ask for a deeper analysis. See more details in the How-To's section further in this chapter.

▶ **Use online resources to estimate cash flow.** To roughly estimate monthly cash flow, use Zillow.com and Redfin.com to estimate monthly liabilities, such as mortgage, tax, and HOA fees vs. potential rental estimates. Zillow.com offers its own Zillow Rent Index and both Zillow.com and Redfin.com offer current lists of similar properties and their current rental rates. Having monthly liabilities and potential monthly rental income at hand, you can roughly estimate if the property makes sense for your needs and whether it deserves further analysis. See more details in the How-To's section further in this chapter.

▸ **Hire a highly experienced real estate agent.** It may take time to find an experienced agent that is effective at both listing and selling. It takes great skill and experience to get a good deal in a highly competitive, smoking-hot market when buying or to generate a steady stream of qualified buyers, resulting in multiple offers, when selling. Incompetence has no place in such high-stakes situations, so hire a pro with a proven track record.

How-To's

HOW-TO: USE ZILLOW.COM TO FIND TARGET PROPERTIES

To identify your target properties using Zillow.com, follow these steps:

1. Navigate to www.zillow.com.
2. Search the target area by providing either the city name or zip code. For example, consider searching Maple Valley, WA.
3. In the menu bar, specify your desired price range. For example, a maximum of $400K.
4. In the menu bar, specify the desired number of bedrooms (or beds). For example, 3+.
5. In the menu bar, check the desired "Home Type." For example, homes that are single-family residences (SFRs).
6. In the menu bar, under the "More" attribute, you can specify more criteria to narrow down the pool of target properties even further. For example, you'll find the age of the house under "Year Built." You may want to set your minimum year at 1979 in order to avoid any houses built when asbestos was in use. Having asbestos in the house is not such a big deal as

long as you inform the renter, as required by law, of its presence and don't disturb it (the asbestos, that is).

7. After selecting all desired criteria, you should see a screen similar to the following:

8. Start clicking on either the dots on the map or the tiles on the right to bring up a preview of the properties. Pick one of the properties you wish to research further, and you should see a view similar to the following:

9. Click through the pictures. Usually, they are professionally produced. If not, you will notice, and it may be a sign of neglect (a bad thing) or, potentially, a distressed property that begs to sell fast, thus potentially promising a larger discount

(a good thing). And finally, it could be a fraudulent post. Pay attention to the details.

10. Review the number of beds and square footage. In the example above, 5 bedrooms on 1,756 sqft would be on the tight end; meaning, some rooms are very small. Remember, though, you are purchasing a property to rent—not for yourself. Think of your target renter and what they would want. Is it a young family with two kids? What else?

11. Scroll down and expand the "Zestimate" section. Zestimate is Zillow's own geek speak on how they appraise the property based on their own internal magic—a secret algorithm based on analyzing thousands, if not millions, of properties they keep in their database. For this property, see the following picture. Notice the Rent Zestimate figure ($2K) and the Zestimate range ($2K-$2.5K). This is probably how much you could charge your potential renter. If the property is relatively new and in great condition, you could probably charge what's displayed (and even on the higher end). On the other hand, if the property is older, then it would be on the lower end of the Rent Zestimate. Remember, though, that market conditions will ultimately dictate what you can charge. If the market is smoking hot, any property will be snatched up very fast—both properties for purchase and for rent. Also, notice the Zestimate forecast; this is how Zillow thinks the property will appreciate within a year. It's not an exact science to say the least, and it's all subject to local conditions. But it's a start, and it gives you a starting point for estimating appreciation—the key driver behind equity and net worth growth.

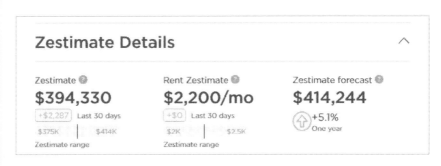

12. Scroll down to the "Price/Tax History" section and expand it. You should see a view similar to the following figure. Notice the date when the property was listed. How long has it been since it was first listed? A property that stays on the market a long time has a better chance of offering a deeper discount, but it may also indicate there are some troubles with it (which are different ways of saying the same thing). Sometimes, it may show a price cut over time—a clear sign of low market temperature, where buyers have the upper hand. Other times, you may see the property went into a pending state and then came back onto the market. This could be due to some contingencies—for example, the buyers decided not to follow through either because they couldn't get financing (bummer for the seller) or because major issues were discovered during the property's inspection. Having problems discovered during inspection doesn't mean you should immediately discard the property; sometimes it means you could request a deeper discount and put in your own sweat equity to fix it. Notice the annual taxes in the following figure. This is important, as this will play a major role when estimating the profitability and potential cash flow of the property.

Price / Tax History   ∧

Price History

DATE	EVENT	PRICE		$/SQFT	SOURCE	
03/10/17	Listed for sale	$385,000	+51.0%	$219	Realty Executi...	⚑
04/27/11	Sold	$255,000		$145	Public Record	⚑

Tax History

Find assessor information on the county website

YEAR	PROPERTY TAXES	CHANGE	TAX ASSESSMENT	CHANGE
2015	$4,661	--	$338,000	+5.3%
2014	$4,661	+10.0%	$321,000	+25.4%

13. Scroll down to the "Neighborhood" section and expand it. You should see a view similar to the following.

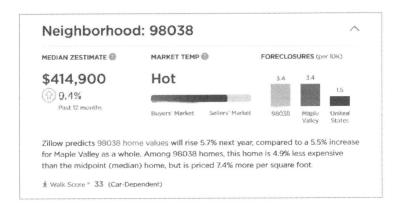

Notice whether the "Market Temp" is hot or cold, or anything in between. If the Market Temp is hot, the property probably will be snatched up very quickly and will go into pending status usually within a week, or even faster. Hot means it's a seller's market, where buyers are desperate to buy and get into bidding wars (sometimes in the high thousands above asking price). I just saw a property that sold $125K over list price, crazy stuff. I even posted about it on my Facebook feed. If the Market Temp is cold, there is an opportunity for a bargain, but usually there is a reason why it's cold. This may be due to no jobs, a high crime rate, low school ratings, long commutes, or other non-flattering reasons. In short, the location is not desired. Be careful about ending up with a property that attracts tenants you'll wish you'd never have dealt with in the first place.

14. Scroll down to the "Nearby Schools" section and expand it. You should see a view similar to the following.

Nearby Schools in Maple Valley   ⌃

SCHOOL RATING		GRADES	DISTANCE
8 out of 10	Lake Wilderness Elementary	PK-5	1.8 mi
9 out of 10	Cedar River Middle	6-7	2.6 mi
7 out of 10	Tahoma Senior High	10-12	3.5 mi

School ratings matter. If you target established families with kids as your potential renters, then chances are they're also looking at the same data on Zillow, and they want the best possible schools their money can rent. Keep in mind that school ratings are based on public reviews and could be easily skewed by a parent who's upset their kid wasn't given a participation trophy, and now they've written a devastating review of the school. Go deeper and review the reviews, and try to see if there's a trend. If the majority are not so great, then the school's rating is probably accurate. But if it's a random helicopter parent, then chances are the school's rating is higher than it appears.

15. Scroll down to the "Similar Homes for Sale" section and expand it. You should see a view similar to the following.

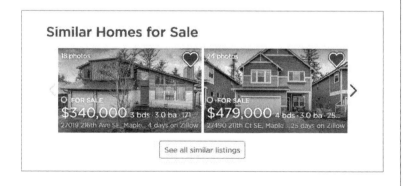

16. Review other similar homes that are currently listed on the market and their prices. It should give you an idea if the asking price of the property in question correlates with the market.

17. If you feel the property resonates with you, click on the "Expand" option in the upper-right corner. This will open the property's page in its own browser window. Copy the link from the address bar of the newly opened browser window and paste it into a document, or someplace where you can collect the list of properties you would like your agent to take you touring after your online research.

18. Call your real estate agent to schedule property tours, and send them a list of the 10 most-promising properties you have collected.

HOW-TO: USE REDFIN.COM TO FIND TARGET PROPERTIES

To identify your target properties using Redfin.com, follow these steps:

1. Navigate to www.redfin.com.
2. Search the target area by providing either the city name or zip code. For example, consider searching Maple Valley, WA.
3. In the filter bar, specify your desired price range. For example, a maximum of $400K.
4. In the filter bar, specify the desired number of bedrooms (or beds). For example, a minimum of 3.
5. In the filter bar, click on "More Filters" to expand it, and specify any additional desired criteria.

6. Under "Property Type," leave the "House" option checked, leave the rest unchecked, and then click on the "Update Search" button.

7. In the filter bar, under the "More Filters" attribute, you can specify more criteria to narrow down the pool of properties even further. For example, you'll find the age of the house under "Year Built." You may want to set your minimum year at 1979 in order to avoid any houses built when asbestos was in use. Having asbestos in the house is not such a big deal as long as you inform the renter, as required by law, of its presence and don't disturb it (the asbestos, that is).

8. After selecting all desired criteria, you should see a screen similar to the following:

9. Start clicking on properties on the map or on list items on the right to bring up a preview of the properties in the upper-right corner. Select one of the properties you wish to research further, and you should see a view similar to the following:

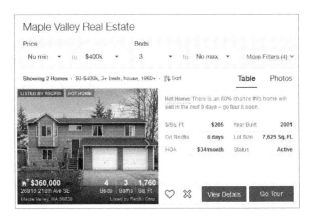

10. Click through the pictures. Usually, they are professionally produced. If not, you will notice, and it may be a sign of neglect (a bad thing) or, potentially, a distressed property that begs to sell fast, thus potentially promising a larger discount (a good thing). And finally, it could be a fraudulent post. Pay attention to the details.

11. Review the number of beds and square footage. In the example above, 4 bedrooms on 1,760 sqft is fairly reasonable, although on the tighter end; meaning, rooms are somewhat small or the halls are narrow. Remember, though, you are purchasing a property to rent—not for yourself. Think of your target renter and what they would want. Is it a young family with two kids? What else?

12. The Redfin estimate is not always available in preview mode—and sometimes not available at all—which makes Zillow a more effective tool for quickly estimating the market value of homes. Redfin is faster to publish properties, however. More often than not, I get notified by my Redfin iPhone app about a property that was just listed, while Zillow takes its time—sometimes days.

13. Click on the "View Details" button; the page should open in a separate window or tab.

14. Click on the "Redfin Estimate" link at the top; the page scrolls down automatically to the "Redfin Estimate" section.

15. Scroll down to the "Property History" section. You should see a view similar to the following.

Property History for 26810 218th Ave SE

Date	Event & Source	Price	Appreciation
Mar 23, 2017	Listed (Active) NWMLS #1092635	$360,000	—
Apr 22, 2015	Sold (Public Records) Public Records	$295,000	>1,000%/yr
Mar 12, 2015	Sold (Public Records) Public Records	$190,000	5.9%/yr
Mar 11, 2015	Delisted NWMLS #677872	—	—
Mar 11, 2015	Sold (MLS) (Sold)	$190,000	

Notice the date when the property was listed. How long has it been since it was first listed? A property that stays on the market a long time has a better chance of offering a deeper discount, but it may also indicate there are some troubles with it (which are different ways of saying the same thing). Sometimes, it may show a price cut over time—a clear sign of low market temperature, where buyers have the upper hand. Other times, you may see the property went into a pending state and then came back onto the market. This could be due to some contingencies—for example, the buyers decided not to follow through either because they couldn't get financing (bummer for the seller) or because major issues were discovered during the property's inspection. Having problems discovered during inspection doesn't mean you should immediately discard the property; sometimes it means you could request a deeper discount and put in your own sweat equity to fix it. Notice the annual taxes in the following figure. This is important, as this will play a major role when estimating the profitability and potential cash flow of the property.

Taxable Value		
Land	$80,000	Taxes (2017)
Additions	$140,000	**$2,922**
Total	$220,000	

16. Scroll down to the "Neighborhood" section and then specifically to "Median Real Estate Values." This is where you can compare this property vs. market metrics such as price per square foot and the sale price to list price ratio. If it's below 100%, then it's a buyers market. If it's above 100%, then the market is hot and bidding wars are on.

Median Real Estate Values			
Location	List Price	$ / Sq. Ft.	Sale / List
98038	$495,250	$209	101.1%
Maple Valley	$535,000	$212	101.0%
King County	$580,000	$288	102.7%

$/Sq. Ft. Houses in 98038

17. Scroll down to the "Nearby Schools" section. You should see a view similar to the following.

School ratings matter. If you target established families with kids as your potential renters, then chances are they're also looking at the same data on Redfin, and they want the best possible schools their money can rent. Keep in mind that school ratings are based on public reviews and could be easily skewed by a parent who's upset their kid wasn't given a participation trophy, and now they've written a devastating review of the school. Go deeper and review the reviews, and try to see if there's a trend. If the majority are not so great, then the school's rating is probably accurate. But if it's a random helicopter parent, then chances are the school's rating is higher than it appears.

18. Scroll down to the "Similar Homes" section. You should see a view similar to the image on the following page. Review other similar homes that are currently listed on the market and those that have recently sold and their prices. This should give you an idea if the asking price of the property in question correlates with the market.

19. Call your real estate agent, send them a list of the 10 most-promising properties you have collected during your online research, and ask your real estate agent to tour them.

HOW-TO: USE ZILLOW.COM TO QUICKLY ESTIMATE CASH FLOW

To quickly estimate cash flow using Zillow.com, follow these steps:

1. Navigate to www.zillow.com.
2. See the previous section, "How-To: Use Zillow.com to Find Target Properties," to identify a property for a quick cash-flow analysis.
3. On the target property page, scroll down to the "Zestimate Details" section. Notice the "Rent Zestimate" value and the "Zestimate range," as shown in the following figure. Newer properties in a desired location may rent for higher than the Rent Zestimate value, while older homes may go for less. Use this value as a starting point, and then consider lowering it and staying on the conservative side of your estimate.

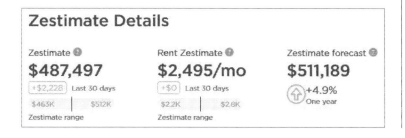

4. Scroll down to the "Mortgages" section, check the "Include taxes/ins." option, and review the "Your payment" value—this is an estimate of your monthly liabilities. Compare your Rent Zestimate vs. monthly liabilities ("Your payment"). If monthly liabilities are lower than the Rent Zestimate, there's a good chance this is a cash-flow property that deserves further analysis.

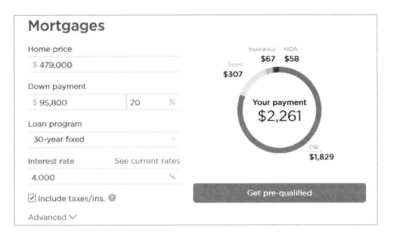

5. Consider playing with the down payment and interest rate and other parameters. For example, if the property isn't cash flowing—meaning, the monthly liabilities are higher than the Rent Zestimate—you may want to increase your down payment to lower the monthly liabilities.

HOW-TO: USE REDFIN.COM TO QUICKLY ESTIMATE CASH FLOW

To quickly estimate cash flow using Redfin.com, follow these steps:

1. Navigate to www.redfin.com.
2. See the previous section, "How-To: Use Redfin.com to Find Target Properties," to identify a property for a quick cash-flow analysis.
3. Next, you'll need to estimate the rental value of the property. Find the "Rental Estimate" section on the Redfin page where you should be able to see a range of comparable rent.

4. On Redfin, scroll down to the "Payment Calculator" and click on "Customize Calculations." Notice the monthly liabilities (payment) estimate at the top:

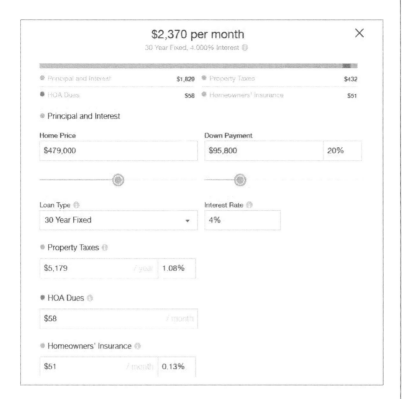

5. Consider playing with the down payment and interest rate and other parameters. For example, if the property isn't cash flowing—meaning, the monthly liabilities are higher than the "Rent Zestimate"—you may want to increase the down payment to lower monthly liabilities.

HOW-TO: USE TRULIA.COM TO QUICKLY EVALUATE THE RENTAL MARKET

To quickly evaluate the rental rates for a particular target market, follow these steps:

1. Navigate to www.trulia.com.

2. Click on "Rent" from the top navigation bar, or choose "Rent" from the drop-down list next to the search box. Type the name of your target market into the search box (we're using

Maple Valley in the example below), and click on the "Search" button:

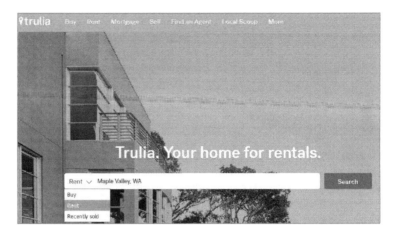

3. On the search results page, narrow down the list of properties by specifying the minimum number of beds (for example, 3), the property type (for example, single-family home), and the square footage. Review the resulting list of properties and their current rental rates (as shown in the following figure) and compare them to the "Rent Zestimate" you obtained earlier from Zillow (from the section titled "How-To: Use Zillow.com to Quickly Estimate Cash Flow.")

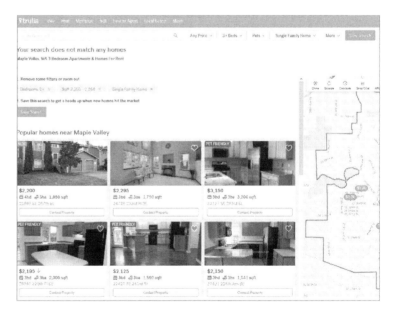

4. Pay attention to the attributes listed for the rental properties, especially to square footage—the results may not show precise numbers. For example, if you are evaluating a 2,200-sqft property and its Rent Zestimate is $2,300 but comparable properties on Trulia.com show listed rental rates of $2,000, you may find out that the properties listed on Trulia have less square footage, which may explain the lower listed rent, so it shouldn't discourage you. You may demand higher rent, as warranted by the larger square footage of the property you offer.

HOW-TO: USE HOTPADS.COM TO QUICKLY EVALUATE THE RENTAL MARKET

To quickly evaluate the rental rates for a particular target market, follow these steps:

1. Navigate to www.hotpads.com.
2. Type the name of your target market into the search box (we're using Maple Valley in the example below).
3. On the search results page, click on the "For rent" menu to expand it, and then select "Houses for Rent" from the drop-down menu. (We want to select houses, as this book focuses on single-family homes, not condos or other types of properties):

4. Specify any additional criteria to narrow down the list of properties. For example, a minimum of 3 beds, the square footage range, and anything else. Review the resulting list of properties and their current rental rates (as shown in the following figure) and compare them to the "Rent Zestimate" you obtained earlier from Zillow (from the section titled "How-To: Use Zillow.com to Quickly Estimate Cash Flow.")

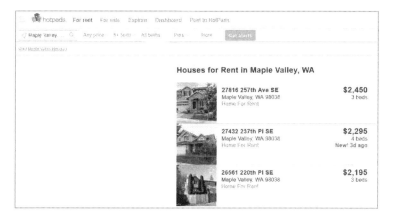

5. Pay attention to the attributes listed for the rental properties, especially to square footage—the results may not show precise numbers. For example, if you are evaluating a 2,200-sqft property and its Rent Zestimate is $2,300 but comparable properties on Hotpads.com show listed rental rates of $2,000, you may find out that the properties listed on Hotpads have less square footage, which may explain the lower listed rent, so it shouldn't discourage you. You may demand higher rent, as warranted by the larger square footage of the property you offer.

CHAPTER 2

Financing

Overview

So, how do we get funding to acquire a property? Is it all cash or 20% down, or any other options in between? Securing funds is key. While your marketing, tenant screening, property management, and tax strategy could be optimal or less so, financing is binary—it's either there or it isn't. For example, you may find a great property in an area where renters are hungry for great rentals due to very low inventory. You call your lender and start working on collecting the paperwork, which, by itself, is tedious and time consuming—and very intrusive with regards to your privacy. Now imagine your disappointment when the lender who helped you so many times cannot help you this time simply because you've hit your debt-to-income (DTI) limits. "But I have enough for a down payment!" you say. The lender responds, "Sorry, the Dodd-Frank Act says I can't."

Among other key things that can derail your efforts is credit score.

LEVERAGE

Property purchased all cash that's valued at $500K and appreciating at the national average of 5% will gain $25K in net worth the first year.

Monthly cash flow will be higher.

Five properties purchased via financing through leverage valued at $500K each, and appreciating at the national average of 5%, will gain $125K total in net worth the first year. Monthly cash flow will be lower or break even. If cash flow is negative, your math is broken. You can refinance and cash out the equity ($125K) to use as a down payment for purchasing another investment property.

Property appreciation isn't taxed until realized (sold).

Lenders lend money based on net worth.

Net worth is increased by both realized money (post-tax) and unrealized appreciation (pre-tax).

A higher credit score increases the chances of loan approval and helps to improve your loan's terms. Lenders love working with financially solid customers, and credit scores are one of their key metrics. Lenders would prefer to deny a loan request and potentially lose revenue vs. approve it only to deal with delinquencies down the road. Luckily, there are ways to control and improve your credit score, all free of charge. Speaking of loan terms, they can vary wildly, but there are ways to quickly research and get a good idea of what's out there.

Finally, one of the most important aspects, if not the most important, is finding a great lender that works with you effectively, efficiently, and patiently.

Not all lenders are made equal. I can firmly state that I will never again touch Lender X, even with a stick wearing rubber gloves! I will omit the lender's name, but I will say it was one of the nation's largest. Never again. What a mess. While the clerks were very polite and cheerful, the whole process—which I ended intentionally after giving them some benefit of the doubt (that evaporated very quickly)—was a disaster. Every time I called, they had no clue who I was or any knowledge of my situation. They asked me multiple times to perform the same tasks and supply the same materials, only to inform me that their fax came out illegible. Fax?! Hello! 21st century!! Email anyone? "Sorry, we don't work with email yet..."

Goodbye.

I switched back to a small and much more focused bank, and since then, I've worked only with them. Phone, email, text, and returning my calls; remembering me and greeting me by name; full awareness of my situation; proactive updates; patiently and thoroughly educating me on the process without confusing geek speak; and timely and flawless execution all the way to closing. And then we repeated the process a few more times—the same friction-free story of success. Ah, heaven... They weren't the cheapest, but the service was worth it, especially when timeliness is key and you need to get the funds by the closing date.

Even if you have plenty of cash to purchase the property without financing, you should consider financing. Leverage is key to growing your net worth exponentially. Put simply, leverage is about accessing more money with less money. In other words, you use other people's money (OPM) and put it to work for you. For example, using your own $100K, you can leverage (borrow) an additional $400K via financing from a lender to acquire a property worth $500K. (Remember Schwarzenegger's story at the beginning of the book?) If you had $500K all cash, you could avoid financing and buy one property. By doing so, you could improve your cash flow dramatically. But that would only make sense if you needed cash today. In my case, I don't need cash today—I have a day job that supports me comfortably. Instead, I would use the $500K at hand to leverage (borrow) $2 million total and purchase five properties, each worth $500K. In fact, I did that. My current outstanding debt is over $2 million, secured by rental properties and paid down by tenants who occupy the properties. To understand the math, see the sidebar on "Leverage" (top of page 28).

Design

Consider the following diagram. You, as an investor, are in the center. You need to familiarize yourself with the loans marketplace and what's available. You need to work with an effective lender of your choice who will take care of your financial needs, and on terms heavily dictated by your credit score. And finally, you need to be aware of your credit score, avoid actions that hurt it, continuously monitor it, and improve it to win better terms with your lender.

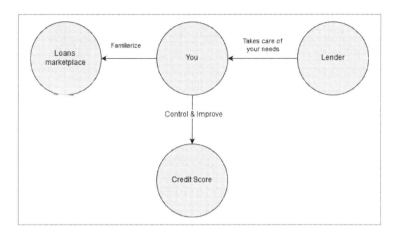

- ▸ **You (investor).** This is you, the investor who needs to secure funds via financing from a great lender on great terms.
- ▸ **Lender.** The lender assesses the borrower's abilities (that's you) based on your credit score and other factors to determine if you are eligible to borrow, and if so, on what terms.
- ▸ **Credit score.** The credit score is something you control and should maintain in top shape in order to qualify for great loan terms with a lender.
- ▸ **Loans marketplace.** Loans are available nationwide via online tools. You'll want to familiarize yourself with what's available so you can manage meaningful negotiations on loan terms with multiple lenders who are eager to win your business, but only to the extent your credit score allows them.

Strategy

The key objective of financing is to secure funding for your investment property on great terms. Consider the following desires and conditions that will guide your actions toward this objective:

1. **Credit score in top shape.** Having your credit score in top shape directly affects your bottom line. Lenders rely on credit

score heavily to determine your loan terms. Consider the following. By quickly looking at Zillow's mortgage rates (https://www.zillow.com/mortgage-rates), it's easy to compare what rates are available for the various credit scores for a property worth $500K with a down payment of 20%. Here's how it breaks down:

- **Credit score of 680-699:** Interest rate of 4.115% with a mortgage of $2,306/month.
- **Credit score of 720-739:** Interest rate of 3.865% with a mortgage of $2,249/month.

That's a difference of $57/month. This could easily tip the scale of positive/negative cash flow. Now what if you have five rentals? That's $300/monoth. See the "Guidelines" section below on how to keep your credit score in top shape.

2. **DTI is no impediment.** DTI, or debt-to-income ratio, tells a lender how much capacity you have to pay back on more debt. See the "Guidelines" section below for more details on DTI. If you hit the DTI threshold with a lender, you won't get your financing even when you have cash for the down payment. Lenders consider a DTI of 45% as a barrier that's usually hard to cross.

3. **Effective and efficient lender.** I can't stress enough how important this is, especially in a highly competitive market. Sometimes it's wise to take a hit on more expensive loan terms vs. working with a nerve-wracking lender or loan broker. (The lender has the money; the broker doesn't, but they sell the mortgage to the lender in the end for servicing.) It will take time to find your perfect lender, and that usually means making a few mistakes and losing out on a few deals. But eventually, you will partner with a great lender and will continue to work with them.

4. **Full awareness of the loans marketplace.** Zillow's mortgage rates page (https://www.zillow.com/mortgage-rates) is a great place to start your research on what options are out there. It offers multiple parameters you can punch in to get a list of

available lenders, usually lender brokers. I worked with a few and it was fine. It also allows you to look at the loan's details, such as estimated monthly payment—a great reference point when estimating your cash flow and shopping for loan terms:

Loan details	Advertising Disclosure
Loan purpose:	Purchase
Loan product:	30 year fixed
Interest rate:	4.375%
APR:	4.423%
Payment (principal & interest):	$1,997
Estimated total payment:	$2,367
Loan amount:	$400,000
Down payment:	$100,000

Concepts

▶ **Cash-out loan.** A cash-out loan is when you decide to take advantage of the equity in your property—either a personal residence or an investment property. In this case, you use the equity in your property to take out a lump sum of hard cash. You start paying down the monthly payments on this cash-out loan's full amount, not on how much you draw, as is the case with HELOC (which we'll discuss in more detail later in this section). For example, if you were able to get a cash-out loan for $50K, you'd get that money in your bank account at once, and you'd start paying a monthly payment on the full $50K amount, similar to paying down a normal mortgage. (A cash-out loan is, in fact, a normal mortgage.)

▶ **Conforming mortgage.** A conforming mortgage is usually limited, to a certain extent, by how much the lender is allowed to lend. This may vary. Until recently, in the State of Washington, it was $417K tops. There are certain strings attached to it that your lender will explain. The main part is that the terms of a conforming mortgage may vary from the terms of a jumbo loan (jumbo loans are allowed to exceed the lender's limit.) For example, let's say you are considering purchasing a property valued at $600K. The lender requires you to put down at least 20% of it, which is $120K. What about the remaining $480K? A conforming loan won't work, as $480K exceeds the $417K limit. You will need to decide whether to go for a jumbo loan (with different loan terms, including a different interest rate) or to put down $183K to qualify for the conforming mortgage.

▶ **Debt-to-income (DTI) ratio.** The debt-to-income (or DTI) ratio is an important metric that tells the lender whether you've reached your financial-credibility threshold. DTI includes all your monthly liabilities, such as mortgage payments, credit cards, and leased car payments. This number is then divided by the total of your monthly income, including your day-job salary and any rental income. (Your lender may decide to only count 75% of your actual rental income to mitigate the risk of potential vacancies and reduce the lender's risk. I told you these guys know a thing or two about risk; love partnering with them.) When you hit the 45-50% threshold, your lender will let you know that your chances of getting additional financing are low at best or non-existent. For example, if you already have a few rental properties financed through mortgages, you many want to first run some numbers with your lenders to discover your DTI before spending time and energy on hunting down additional properties. Regardless of whether you have enough money for a down payment, if you hit your DTI limit with the lender, you need to work on reducing your debt (say, by selling off one of the properties—ideally, the one that's appreciated well or isn't performing as desired). You could also generate more income—for example, increasing the rent, taking on a new job, or starting a side hustle (like creating a digital product and selling it online similar to this book you're reading).

▶ **Down payment.** You need to have some money to purchase a property. It could be as low as a few percent—both FHA (Federal Housing Administration) and non-government financial institutions offer a 3%-only down payment, and the rest is financed. In low down-payment scenarios, you either need to pay mortgage insurance (which easily could be hundreds of dollars monthly) or find another qualified means of securing your debt. The lenders or authorities deem this necessary with low down payments to ensure you are taking on a reasonable debt that you are capable of paying back. These low down-payment options are usually only available for properties that are for personal residence. However, this doesn't mean you can't take advantage of them as an investor. For example, you could purchase a property and rent out part of it. You could also wait a year or two until the property appreciates and take out a HELOC or cash-out loan to use as a down payment to purchase another property. For investment properties, a 20% down payment is usually the minimum you would need to bring to the table before asking for financing.

▶ **Escrow.** The term "escrow" is used in two situations. The first is when you are in the process of purchasing a property. An escrow company is where you send your earnest money (this is part of the down payment, which could be 10% of purchase price, $10K, or as agreed). In this case, an agent for the escrow company coordinates the whole process between all the parties—seller, buyer, agents, insurance, lenders, authorities, and probably a few more. Another situation when you'll hear the term "escrow" is when you set up your financing, loan, or mortgage via a lender. A lender will ask you whether you'd like to have an escrow account. This is an account, usually managed by the lender, which collects additional funds from you—mainly for the purpose of paying property taxes and insurance on your behalf. I usually ask the lender what's beneficial from a loan-terms perspective—escrow or no. If there's no difference, I go without escrow. This means I will pay the property taxes and property insurance myself; a much better situation since I control my money. I once had a bad experience where I needed to prove to the escrow people a mistake they had made, and then it took months to get my money back. As of this writing, I have another case where a lender told me they'd paid my property taxes while the county's website shows it's still due. Turns out they paid my money to a tax parcel that doesn't exist. Another lender I've crossed from my list. I have a great insurance agent who manages all my insurances—personal and business, real estate, cars, and umbrella—and I get a discount since I am bundling. Property taxes—no worries. Local authorities will let you know exactly how much you owe and how and when to pay it. No escrow accounts for me anymore!

▸ **FHA mortgage.** An FHA mortgage is a government-sponsored program to help increase homeownership. The key to the program is that it only requires a 3% down payment and the rest is financed. The caveat is that it usually requires mortgage insurance (MI), which can easily cost an additional few hundred dollars a months. Bite off only what you can chew—higher financing means higher monthly payments. Plus, a few hundred dollars in MI may be a deal breaker for your cash flow adventure. There are other non-government programs that offer low down-payment financing. You may consider FHA or other low down-payment financing for your personal residence, which will allow you to save money that can be used for a rental property down payment.

▸ **HELOC.** A home equity line of credit, or HELOC, is a line of credit (similar to a credit card) that's secured by your property's equity. Usually, it can only go up to 80% of the property's value. For example, if you own a house appraised at $500K and your mortgage balance is $200K, then the maximum HELOC you could have is $500K*80%-$200K = $200K. $200K is how much credit you could have once approved.

The interesting thing is that it's a line of credit and you can use it similarly to a credit card—whoa! A credit card with a $200K limit. You can use it for whatever purposes you want. Don't use a HELOC for consumer spending, as you would normally use a credit card. The smarter way to use a HELOC is for a down payment to purchase an investment property with a positive cash flow. Usually, the minimum monthly payment for a HELOC is interest only, so it's a lower monthly liability, yet the principal stays the same. For example, let's say you're purchasing a rental property valued at $500K. You use $100K from a HELOC obtained from your personal residence for the down payment, and the remaining $400K you finance through the same lender or a different one. The HELOC is secured by your personal residence, and the rest is secured by the rental property. Effectively, you've purchased an investment property with no money whatsoever—everything is financed. Obviously, the monthly liabilities for both loans (the HELOC and the mortgage) as well as the taxes and insurance should be offset by rent; otherwise, your numbers are broken and you'll end up with negative cash flow. That said, you still have another $100K left from the HELOC, remember? In the example above, you'll recall that you qualified for $200K of HELOC, but you only used $100K for the down payment. So, how about another rental property? At this point, you may hit your DTI limit, which can prevent you from obtaining more financing. But other than DTI, you're good, and you may decide to go for it. I did.

▶ **Jumbo mortgage.** A jumbo loan is a loan that allows you to go above the limits usually imposed on conforming loans. For example, in the State of Washington, it's $417K. The loan terms will vary for conforming vs. jumbo. Review both with your lender. For example, let's say you are considering purchasing an investment property valued at $600K. The lender requires putting down no less than 20%, which is $120K. But how do you finance the remaining $480K? You couldn't go for a conforming loan, as the limit is $417K. So, your options would be to either put down a larger down payment or go for a jumbo loan. Remember, the larger the loan, the higher the monthly liabilities, and this could constrain your cash flow, which, at a minimum, should be break even—not negative. You don't want to finance your investment with your day-job salary on a monthly basis, right?

▶ **Mortgage.** A mortgage is a bank loan secured by real estate. If you default on your payments, the bank may take possession of the property, regardless of whether it's titled to an LLC or not. The mortgage is personally signed by you, so it's a personal guarantee, not the LLC's.

▶ **Mortgage broker.** A mortgage broker is usually a person who sells mortgages but does not service them; rather, they resell the mortgages to financial institutions. For example, you may find a good deal on a mortgage and go for it. You receive a letter asking for payment to go to Company X, but then next month, Big Bank sends you a similar letter also asking for payment on the mortgage. It's okay, you probably just missed the letter where Company X informed you the mortgage was sold to Big Bank, who will be servicing your loan going forward. One important part is to make sure during tax season to get tax documents, usually Form 1098, from both Company X and Big Bank. Since both parties charged you interest on the loan, you will use the total of the interest paid to both parties and write that off from your taxable income to reduce your tax liability. Be sure to get Form 1098 from both parties; they usually send it as required by law after year end and before tax season.

▶ **Mortgage insurance** (**MI**). Mortgage insurance, or MI, is an additional monthly payment usually charged for low down-payment mortgages, such as FHA, which is government sponsored. MI can easily be a few hundred dollars monthly. The trade off is that you can get in the game with only a 3% down payment, but monthly liabilities will be higher due to the larger loan size (the loan will be larger because it includes the MI). Run your numbers—monthly liabilities vs. rental cash flow. If they at least break even, there's a good chance for a successful deal.

▶ **Mortgage lender.** The mortgage lender is the guy with the money. Usually, this is a bank or credit union. Mortgages can be offered and sold in one of two ways. The first is by a broker who doesn't lend the money directly but is excellent at marketing and selling mortgages. The mortgage broker then sells the mortgage to a mortgage lender for servicing (charging you monthly). The second way mortgages can be sold is by the lender itself. In this case, there is no resale of the mortgage. One thing I noticed working with mortgage brokers is that there's an extra step involved—finding a lender who is willing to purchase the mortgage. This isn't a huge risk, but it may prolong the closing period, which could be a bit sensitive at a times and nerve-wracking under time pressure.

▶ **Personal guarantee.** Lenders lend to you personally. Even if you manage real estate properties via legal entities, such as an LLC (discussed further in the "Legal Entity Structure" chapter), the lender won't lend it to your business entity; they will lend it to you personally. The title of the property may (and should) be transferred to the LLC after the purchase to take advantage of the asset protection the LLC offers (again, more on this later).That said, the loan will still be in your name personally. If the bank comes after your property, the LLC won't help here. The LLC protects you against attacks from... Argh, skip to the diagram found in the "Design" section within "Legal Entity Structure" for clarity on it.

Guidelines

▶ **Ask when hard credit inquiries are run.** Many sales promotions may have hidden credit inquiries which usually hurt your credit score. When in doubt, ask if it involves running your credit score. If so, you may need to weigh the pros and cons of moving forward. For example, if you decide to finance your mattress purchase because the deal they offer is irresistible (I just did that), you may want to reconsider it in light of an upcoming property purchase that you will be financing. Either postpone your new mattress purchase or buy it without financing. This will prevent an unnecessary credit inquiry, which will help you keep your credit score in top shape for the near future. To summarize: Credit score inquiries hurt your credit score. Know in advance when they are run, and avoid multiple runs as much as possible.

▶ **Close early in the month.** When buying a property, setting your closing date early in the month has a great advantage, as most mortgage lenders allow a full calendar month before requiring you to start paying down the loan. For example, if you close on January 5th, the earliest the lender will start charging you is March 1st. That's almost two months without having to pay the largest portion of liabilities—the mortgage. This payment gap is very helpful while you work hard to spruce up the property and find qualified tenants. On top of that, lenders usually have a 15-day grace period; meaning, the latest you could start paying is March 15th—giving you more than two months to do your homework (pun intended).

▶ **Don't open a new credit line or request an increase before applying for a major loan.** Changes to lines of credit—new lines or increases to existing ones—will result in hard inquiries to credit score bureaus such as Experian, TransUnion, and Equifax. Such inquiries temporarily hurt your credit score, which could be detrimental should you need a major loan in the foreseeable future for purchasing investment property. This could cause your terms to be worse, or it may cause your loan application to be declined.

▶ **Don't quit your day job, yet.** You may do well with real estate investing to the point where you may consider quitting your day job. Don't do it yet. Lenders feel more comfortable lending to those with W-2s and paystubs vs. those who don't. Keep your day job at least for financing purposes (plus other benefits such as regular paychecks and healthcare).

▶ **Increase your credit limit.** Every six months, consider increasing the credit limit on existing credit cards. While keeping your purchasing habits in check, this will lower your credit card utilization overall—a good driver for credit score improvement. At first, right after the increase to the credit line, your credit score may suffer (due to hard inquiries into credit monitoring bureaus). However, it should bounce back quickly—and even improve—assuming all other good credit habits are in place. Avoid increasing the line of credit before a major loan request; at which time, the credit score needs to be in top shape to win great loan terms (let alone get approved).

▶ **Keep your credit card utilization below 30%.** Utilization simply means the percentage of your total available credit you have used—which you should keep below 30%. Doing so is the most impactful factor in determining whether you qualify for a loan and how attractive the terms will be (other than delinquencies or bankruptcies). Plus, it's the easiest credit score metric you can control.

▶ **Monitor your credit score.** Many credit card companies offer free FICO credit scores on their websites. Use it, it's free. Consider signing up for CreditKarma.com. I personally use it and I like it a lot. CreditKarma.com offers credit scores from the TransUnion and Equifax credit monitoring companies. It also offers great insights and tips on how to improve your credit score. Their monetization is through ads, be advised. More info on this below in the section titled "How-To: Control Your Credit Score Using CreditKarma.com."

▶ **Sign up for more credit cards.** Consider signing up for more credit cards during your downtime when you're not anticipating any active property investing and when you don't expect to apply for a loan. More credit cards means a higher credit limit, while your purchasing habits should stay the same. It will result in lower credit card utilization over-all, preferably well below 30%. Many cards don't require an annual fee and offer bonus cashback, miles, and other perks for free. Be aware that opening a new credit card will hurt your credit score temporarily, which is not a big deal at all. That's the reason to avoid opening new credit lines before a major loan request to keep your credit score in top shape at that specific time.

▸ **Spread out your credit card utilization.** After signing up for new credit cards, make sure they are utilized at some level. Credit score monitoring bureaus like to see some utilization. Consider setting up auto-payment for Netflix, Hulu, HBO, or other utilities you may have using different cards. The cards will show utilization—great!—and it's low maintenance since it's on autopilot. Going further, you may decide to use your Costco Visa card only when shopping at Costco, your AMEX when at grocery stores and everywhere else, and your Alaska Miles Visa as a fall back where AMEX is not accepted (small businesses usually don't accept AMEX for its high fees). Only three credit cards total in your wallet—not a big deal at all—but it helps maintain continuous utilization and improve your credit score overall, which will enable you to score better loan terms when applying for investment property mortgages.

How-To's

HOW-TO: USE ZILLOW.COM TO COMPARE MORTGAGE RATES

To compare available mortgage rates using Zillow.com, follow these steps:

1. Navigate to https://www.zillow.com/mortgage-rates/.
2. On the left-hand side, fill in basic criteria, such as purchase price, down payment, and credit score, and then click on the "Advanced" link. More options will appear, similar to the following:

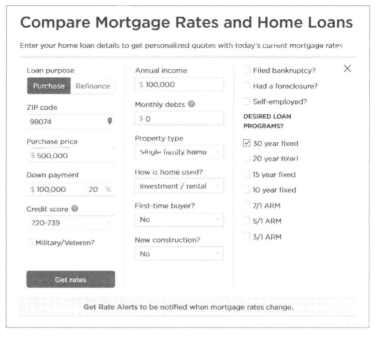

3. Specify additional criteria, such as "Property type," "How is home used?," and "DESIRED LOAN PROGRAMS?," and then click on the "Get rates" button. You should see a view similar to the following:

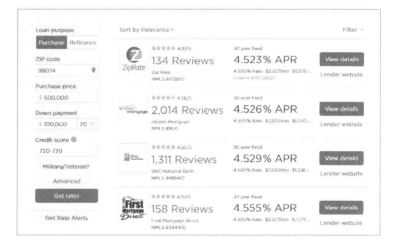

4. Click on the "Sort by Relevance" link and choose "Rate" to see the lowest rates available. (Remember, lower rates come with the expense of higher upfront fees.) Observe the rates:

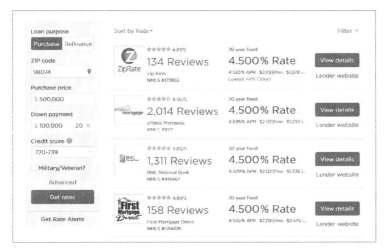

5. Click on the "Sort by Rate" link and choose "Fees" to sort by lowest fees:

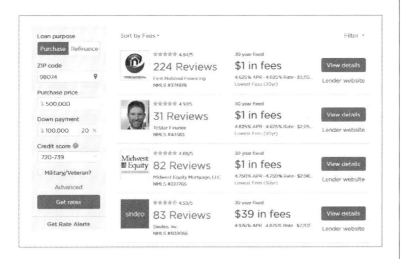

6. Click on the "Sort by Fees" link and choose "Monthly Payment" to sort by lowest monthly payment, usually directly related to rates:

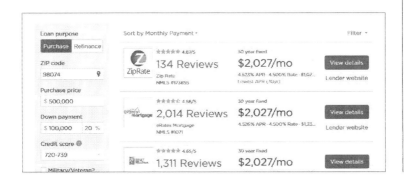

7. Click on the "Filter" link, choose the relevant options you are interested in, and then click on the "Filter" button. Usually, a 30-year-fixed loan is most suitable for investment properties (since you want to reduce monthly liabilities). This helps you to get to a positive cash-flow state by spreading out the payments over the longest possible time span:

LOAN PROGRAMS	LOAN TYPES	POINTS
☑ 30 year fixed	☑ Conforming	☐ No fees, no points
☐ 20 year fixed	☐ Jumbo	☑ 0 points
☐ 15 year fixed	☐ FHA	☐ 1 point
☐ 10 year fixed	☐ VA	☐ 2 points
☐ 7/1 ARM	☐ Balloon	☐ More than 2 points
☐ 5/1 ARM	☐ Interest-only	
☐ 3/1 ARM	☐ HARP	

Filter

8. Observe the resulting loans.
9. Click on the "View Details" button to review the estimated fees. This is a one-time payment you will need to consider. The main thing to look at is "Lender credit." This is something you can negotiate (ask for an increase) when discussing the terms with the lender or loan broker. It's not uncommon when the lender offers lender credit that it offsets the underwriting fees altogether (but not in the example below):

Estimated fees

Appraisal fee:	$475
Underwriting fee:	$995
Lender credit:	*($392)*
Total Estimated Fees:	**$1,078**

Third party fees may not be included.

10. At this point, you have a good understanding of the available rates for your credit score range, the monthly payment (to roughly estimate monthly liabilities), and the one-time fees related to getting the financing. Keep in mind that some of the fees could be financed into the loan itself, and, when spread over 30 years, these fees would be negligible and wiped out as an upfront fee. I usually take advantage of this option.

11. Collect a few offerings that look reasonable to you and directly submit an application via Zillow.com. After which, you will receive a confirmation email and probably a call within 10 minutes from the rep to discuss the terms. Alternatively, you can take the offerings to your local lender and ask them if they can beat the terms you have on hand.

HOW-TO: CONTROL YOUR CREDIT SCORE USING CREDITKARMA.COM

To control your credit score using CreditKarma.com, follow these steps:

1. Navigate to https://www.creditkarma.com/.
2. Sign up for free access.
3. From the navigation bar, click on "Overview," and then select "My Overview" from the left-hand side menu to navigate to the dashboard. You should see a view similar to the following:

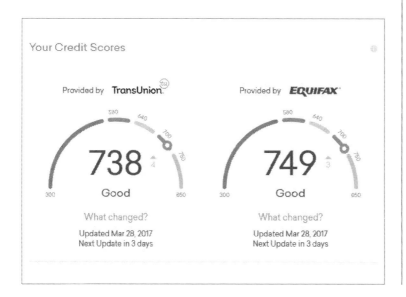

4. Notice the scores. TransUnion is at 738, and Equifax is at 749 —a good thing! Now click on the "What changed?" link.

5. Review the changes and what caused the change, as shown in the following figure:

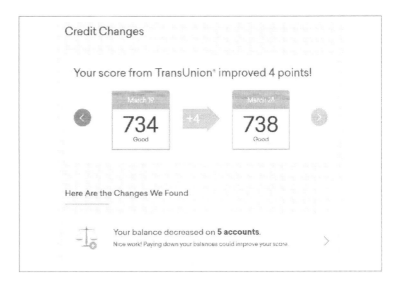

6. On the left-hand side, click on the "Credit Factors" link, and review the factors that impact your credit score the most. You should see a view similar to the following:

What can impact my score?	TransUnion	EQUIFAX	
Credit Card Utilization ⚡ High Impact The amount of your total available credit that you're using. See details.	7%	7%	>
Payment History ⚡ High Impact The percentage of payments you've made on time. See details.	100%	100%	>
Derogatory Marks ⚡ High Impact The number of collection accounts, bankruptcies, foreclosures, civil judgments or tax liens on your report. See details.	0	0	>
Age of Credit History ⚡ Medium Impact The average length of time your accounts have been open. See details.	1 Yr, 8 Mos ▲	1 Yr, 10 Mos ▲	>
Total Accounts ⚡ Low Impact The total number of open and closed accounts on your report. See details.	23	24	>
Credit Inquiries ⚡ Low Impact The number of "hard pulls" on your credit report for things like new credit applications in the last two years. See details.	11	10	>

7. Notice what factors make the most impact and which less so. Credit card utilization appears to be the most impactful, yet it's the easiest to control, making it the best avenue to quickly improve your overall credit score. See the "Guidelines" section earlier in this chapter for more on how to make quick fixes to your credit score by applying credit card best practices.

8. Click on the "See details" link beneath each factor to learn more about how to make your credit score shine and grow.

9. Consider downloading the CreditKarma mobile app to monitor your credit score on the go.

CHAPTER 3

Marketing

Overview

So, how do we target and find friction-free tenants and close the deal? Good tenants will keep the property in great shape and will pay the rent on time. These two items are the most important.

Marketing is about finding great tenants, verifying what they claim about themselves (via screening within legal boundaries), and making sure they qualify per your standards. Finally, the marketing process ends with signing the lease and other key papers, getting the rent and security deposit, and exchanging the keys. Happy tenants, happy landlord—and vice versa.

Design

Consider the following diagram. You, as the investor and owner of the single-family rental home, need to attract great tenants via online advertising, where prospects are looking for rental properties. You also need to screen those who apply within legal boundaries and qualify them based on your own standards (for example, criminal records, undesired financial behavior, lack of great recommendations, and more):

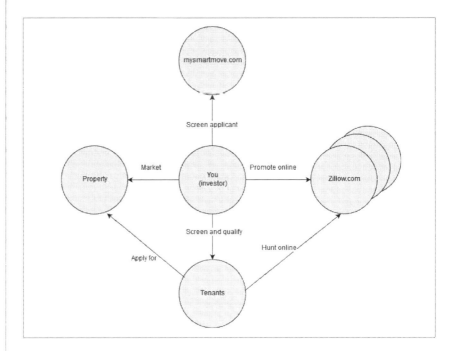

- ▶ **You (investor).** You want to market your property online to highly qualified tenants, screen them based on qualifications, and get them to sign the lease.
- ▶ **Zillow.com, etc.** The Zillow Group owns several of the top websites, including Zillow.com, Trulia.com, and Hotpads. com. You can post your advertisement for free on Zillow, which then promotes it on all three websites.
- ▶ **Tenants.** Prospective tenants who find your property while shopping online on Zillow.com, Trulia.com, and Hotpads. com can submit a request for more info or for a showing. You take applications and then screen them via TransUnion's MySmartMove online tool (more on this later) and other means. Finally, you sign a lease with highly qualified tenants.
- ▶ **Property.** You own and market your property to highly qualified tenants who apply for rent.

Strategy

Consider the following key objectives at this stage of marketing:

1. Generate demand for your property among desired prospective tenants. This is usually done in certain specific ways when advertising the rental property online. For example, one key factor could be requiring a certain credit score level upfront to make sure only highly qualified prospective tenants apply.

2. Clear qualification will help prevent non-qualifying prospective tenants from submitting inquiries or applications while allowing qualifying prospective tenants to move to the next stage of screening.

3. Streamline the application submission and

4. Assessment process via online tools.

5. Prepare ready-to-go documents that are easy to read and understand, yet comprehensive. This will streamline the lease signature process while covering all key aspects of the lease, including the obligations and rights of both tenant and landlord. (A great library of document templates is included in *The Book on Rental Property Investing*; see Resources.)

6. Sign lease agreements efficiently and move on to the next deal. The lease signing is a high-adrenaline procedure for both the landlord and prospective tenant. The less friction, the more pleasant the process of signing goes, resulting in both parties happily exchanging keys for deposits.

Concepts

▶ **Adverse action.** Whenever you need to turn down an applicant who applied for your property, you may be required by local law to send a rejection letter, called an adverse action letter. Templates are available either on TransUnion's MySmartMove.com or with the purchase of *The Book on Rental Property Investing*. I use the forms that come with the book.

▶ **Application.** Prospective tenants express their desire to rent by filling out a rental application. This is a form you provide either by sending it to them electronically or by handing out a printout when the tenant comes for a property showing. The application serves two purposes: First, it informs the prospective tenant what qualifying standards they need to meet to qualify. Second, it captures key information about the prospective tenant that you, as a landlord, will use to verify the prospective tenant's claims about themselves in order to qualify. Templates are available with the purchase of *The Book on Rental Property Investing*. I use the forms that come with the book.

▸ **Background check.** A background check should be performed by a third party specializing in the field. I use TransUnion's MySmartMove.com, which is very convenient. You should run a background check on all prospective tenants over the age of 18 who will be living on the property. The background check will verify the credit score and financial strength of the tenant and any legal entanglements with authorities, if any, including registered sex offenses and other violations. The MySmartMove.com website will take a $35 non-refundable fee per application from the tenant. Once paid, it will produce a report that is available for you, the landlord, for review. See more details in the "How-To's" subsection down below.

▸ **Deposit to hold.** A deposit to hold when renting is similar to earnest money when purchasing a home. It helps to avoid a situation where the prospective tenant gets cold feet and never moves in after asking you to hold the property for them for a few more days before signing the contract. In the meantime, you, as a landlord, lost time (rent, money), and other prospective tenants who were interested in the property may have already rented elsewhere (opportunity cost). When signing a lease where the move-in isn't the same day, consider taking a deposit to hold the property, and forfeit it in case of a no-show. Templates are available with the purchase of *The Book on Rental Property Investing*. I use the forms that come with the book.

▶ **Lease agreement.** A lease agreement is the contract between the tenant and a landlord on the terms of the rent. It captures basic information, such as each party's details, the cost of the rent, the time of move in, and the responsibilities of both parties. This is where signatures go, and this is the time when the deposit is made and the keys are exchanged. This is a win-win. The tenant gets a place to stay and the landlord gets paid. Templates are available with the purchase of *The Book on Rental Property Investing*. I use the forms that come with the book.

▶ **Qualification standards.** This concept is heavily emphasized in *The Book on Rental Property Investing*, and I have gladly adopted their standards. Besides the obvious standards—like a credit score of a certain level and absolutely no criminal records—I also liked the one that states the prospective tenant needs to show proof of income that's three times the rent. If not, no one will enjoy the partnership—neither the landlord nor the tenant. Templates are available with the purchase of *The Book on Rental Property Investing*. I use the forms that come with the book.

▶ **Security deposit.** A security deposit serves as "insurance" in case the tenant leaves the premises in a state less than desired, as per the lease agreement. For example, the tenant may leave something broken that would require a handyman to fix or an unpaid water bill that comes due. Local laws require the landlord to return the security deposit within two weeks after the tenant moves out (less any deductions due to unfulfilled obligations). Your local laws may vary.

Guidelines

▶ **Batch showing.** When you publish your rental property online, you will start getting inquiries via email and phone asking for a showing. Set the showing for a specific day and batch all interested prospects at the same time. You will hit two birds with one stone. Your time is very valuable, and, by doing one showing, you will save a ton of time. This is especially useful for no-shows. Second, prospective tenants will witness the demand—healthy competition is great for business, and it drives a faster closing (and at better terms). Bring several application printouts to hand out, or ask for emails to send the electronic version. Follow up after the showing to encourage prospects to apply while the showing residue is still warm.

▶ **Conduct a background check for potential renters.** Running a background check

▶ **isn't optional.** You want tenants who are financially strong and who will keep your property in top shape. While the background check may not indicate whether the prospective tenant will do that, it may well indicate that they won't. For example, the background check may show no criminal records and no late payments on credit cards. A very good sign; required but not sufficient. On the other hand, if the background check shows multiple delinquencies, let alone bankruptcies (got that once), it's a show stopper, hands down, no more information needed. Simply send the adverse action letter as required by law and thank them for applying. Passing an online background check isn't sufficient in and of itself to qualify a prospect (only a low bar is needed to pass). This is why you'll want to establish some of your own qualification standards (noted in the next bullet). I use MySmartMove.com by TransUnion for the background check online. Additional templates are available with the purchase of *The Book on Rental Property Investing*. I use the forms that come with the book.

▶ **Establish and emphasize qualification standards upfront.** This is a great way to set expectations early to avoid unpleasant surprises down the road. If a prospective tenant is informed early on that they'll need to provide proof of income that's three times the rent, they may decide not to proceed with the application, saving themself the $35 application fee and time for both of you. Templates are available with the purchase of *The Book on Rental Property Investing*. I use the forms that come with the book.

▸ **Read the lease contract jointly.** When both parties (the prospective tenant and the landlord) are ready to sign, make sure to go over the lease together. No need to read it jointly out loud; instead, call out each key section and explain in plain English what it means.

▸ **Renter's insurance.** Make sure the renter has renter's insurance. You rent out a home, not the contents. If something happens to the tenant's stuff, as a landlord, you shouldn't be liable; it should be covered by renter's insurance. Otherwise, if something happens and your insurance company gets a claim, your property insurance rates will go up—not good for cash flow.

▸ **"Sell or be sold."** I adopted this phrase from Grant Cardone, who has a book by the same name—*Sell or Be Sold*. You are running a business, not a sanctuary. "You won't get what you deserve, you'll get what you negotiate" is another line I adopted from Grant. This doesn't mean you need to be a stone-cold maniac, all it means is that if the deal doesn't make sense, then you need to walk away from it—not give in and lose money. It's a free market; supply and demand rules, with a good dose of dignity that goes both ways.

▸ **Turn down non-qualifying prospects.** If the prospective tenant doesn't meet either of the qualifying standards, turn them down. Be well aware of non- discrimination laws; this should be straightforward. You may need to send an adverse action letter when turning down an applicant. Qualifying standards you put forward are there for a reason. Use them. For example, proof of income that's three times the rent is another good standard, usually supported by the last few paystubs. Employment verification is another standard procedure, as is recommendation by their supervisor. Templates are available with the purchase of *The Book on Rental Property Investing*. I use the forms that come with the book.

How-To's

HOW-TO: ADVERTISE FOR RENT ON ZILLOW.COM, TRULIA.COM, AND HOTPADS.COM

To publish your property for rent on Zillow.com, Trulia.com, and Hotpads.com, follow these steps:

1. Navigate to www.zillow.com.
2. Create your free account and sign in.
3. Hover over the "Rent" link in the top navigation menu. You should see a view similar to the following:

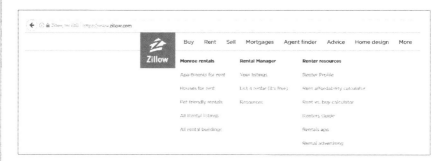

4. In the "Rental Manager" section, click on "List a rental (it's free)."
5. Fill in the required details at a minimum (identified by an asterisk [*] next to it), and click on the "Save and Continue" button:

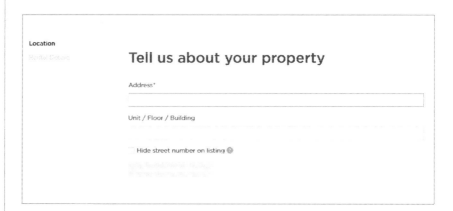

6. Continue filling in the required and optional information as desired to make the property stand out.

7. Once the property is activated, it will appear on all three websites—Zillow.com, Trulia.com, and Hotpads.com—since all of them belong to the Zillow Group:

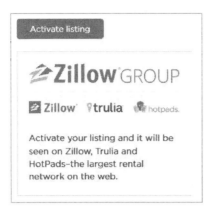

8. Once the property is activated, prospective tenants searching on these websites will see your listing and will be contacting you via phone or email with their information and asking for a showing.

HOW-TO: CONDUCT A BACKGROUND CHECK OF POTENTIAL RENTERS USING TRANSUNION'S MYSMARTMOVE.COM

To conduct a background check of potential renters using TransUnion's MySmartMove.com, follow these steps:

1. Navigate to www.mysmartmove.com.
2. Create your free account and sign in.
3. On the left-hand side, create your property and fill in the required information. Click the "Save" button when finished:

4. On the left-hand side, click on "Start an Application." Select your property, fill in the applicant's email, and choose the "Renter will pay for services" option. Then click on the "Save" button:

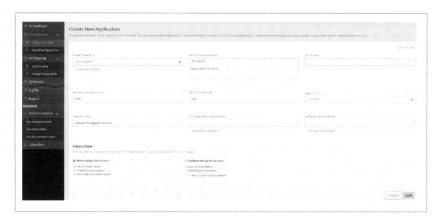

5. The prospective tenant will receive an email notification guiding them through the process of payment and the rest of the steps.

6. Once the prospective tenant has filled in all required information and paid, you, as a landlord, will receive an email notification that the background check is complete and ready for your review.

7. You will be provided with a recommendation based on TransUnion's criteria. You may adopt it or not. Thoroughly review financial, criminal, and other records. If everything is nice and clean, you can move on to further evaluate the prospective tenant based on provided paystubs, as well as references from their supervisor and previous landlord. But if you notice red flags like open bankruptcies, as shown in the example below, waste no time and decline. Chances are TransUnion will recommend so as well:

8. Remember, when declining, you may need to send an adverse action letter. See *The Book on Rental Property Investing* for more details. The book comes loaded with document templates, including this one. I use them.

CHAPTER 4

Property Management

Overview

So, how do you maintain your property in top shape—friction free—optimizing around expenses, time, and personal energy? One option is to hire a property management company and supposedly forget about property management worries at all. That well may be a good approach when you have multiple properties that economically justify such an expense. But when starting out, it's hardly a viable approach. On one end, the goal of property management is to keep the tenant happy; on the other, you also need to stand your ground firmly if the tenant wrongly assumes they've just checked into a hotel and the landlord is the room service receptionist.

Design

Consider the following diagram. You, as the investor, want to keep the tenant happy, the property in good shape, and, most importantly, control your cash flow so that it stays positive and never negative.

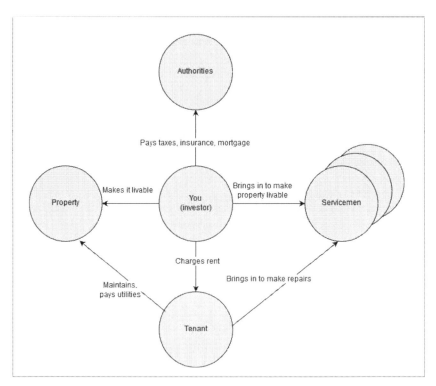

- ▶ **You (investor).** You, as the investor, want to keep your tenant, the authorities, and your creditors happy and the property in good shape. You charge the tenant monthly rent.
- ▶ **Servicemen.** You may bring in servicemen to assess the repairs needed for the property and then to perform the service itself. Servicemen's work is paid by either the landlord or the tenant according to the terms of the lease agreement.
- ▶ **Tenant.** The tenant maintains the property in top shape, pays you monthly rent, pays for utilities, and brings in servicemen to fix what's considered their responsibility, as defined in the lease agreement.
- ▶ **Property.** The property is kept in top shape and paid for by the tenant as per the lease agreement.
- ▶ **Authorities.** This includes local taxes, property insurance, the lender, HOA, and other monthly liabilities that are paid by the landlord (that's you).

Strategy

The key objective of property management is to control and grow your cash flow and your property's appreciation. Consider the following desires and conditions:

1. **Appreciation growth.** You are in this for the long term. Appreciation is a gauge of how well the property performs over time in terms of equity growth. You can use the equity in a couple of ways. First, you can sell the property (realized income) and collect the hard cash just like you would with stocks, including paying a 15% capital gains tax (although that may be fully and legally avoided—not evaded!—by utilizing a few well-known techniques if properly planned ahead). If the property appreciates fast (seller's market), you may consider offloading the property to serve other objectives you may have. Be mindful of depreciation recapture, however (more on this in the "Tax Strategy" chapter). If the property's appreciation performance is sluggish, you may decide to hold it longer (remember buy and hold?) and sell it potentially at a break-even price (if not at a loss) to avert even more losses down the road. Your second option is to use the equity you've built up to refinance (or refi) the property and use this equity as a down payment for another investment property. This is a more common use of the equity that results from property appreciation. Appreciation growth is key to building wealth and your net worth.

2. **Positive cash flow.** Monthly cash flow must be at least $1, never in the red. If in the red, it will hurt your current lifestyle. Lifestyle is important and there is only so much one can tolerate in terms of a lifestyle change. Run your numbers again and adjust them to make them work. If you have spare cash, you may consider paying down more on the loan to lower monthly liabilities. You may increase the rent, with a clear understanding that it may alienate the tenant and make them leave. There are ways to make it less painful, though. You may go to the county assessor and argue that property

taxes are too high and ask them to be reduced. Look at the liabilities and shave a dollar or two from each to get the cash flow back to black and out of red.

3. **The property is kept in top shape.** The initial screening process should have been a good indicator of whether the tenant was a great candidate who will take good care of the property. The lease agreement adds legal language to the contract, and the security deposit adds monetary weight. Even with all the formal safeguards in place, it's worth it to pay a visit once in a while to the property (with a proper heads up to the tenant, as required by the contract) to make sure the property is still in solid shape. Eventually, you will need to rent it out again (or sell it) once the current tenant moves out, and you'll want to do this with minimal investment required to get it spruced up and rentable/sellable again.

4. **The tenant and landlord are happy.** Truth be told, both the tenant and landlord want to hear from one another as little as possible. Ideally, the tenant sets up bill pay on their bank's website, which automatically sends the check to cover rent every month, while enjoying the property and minding their own business. Meanwhile, the landlord never bothers the tenant while getting the rent every month (assuming the property is taken care of and kept in top shape). Ah... heaven. The reality is, in fact, not that far from this. If the tenants were screened properly in the first place, and if the property is new and not falling apart (or has been recently fixed), then both the tenant and the landlord are pretty close to the ideal situation and very much happy. There are always some friction points, especially in the beginning when both parties learn to work together on how to maintain the property; but after that, it's smooth sailing. As long as both parties work with one another, any real-life situations can be easily handled with dignity and mutual respect of each other's interests.

Concepts

- **Property improvement.** Property improvement is a specialized term that shouldn't be used lightly. If you, as a landlord, plan to make changes to the property, it may come in two forms: Property improvement or repairs and maintenance. Changing air filters is repairs and maintenance; changing carpets is not, it's property improvement. Although it may already be obvious, property improvement is something that adds value long term, while repairs and maintenance is not. How you report these expenses on your tax return is important. Repairs and maintenance are normal expenses that could be written off all at once, while property improvement must be depreciated over time—meaning, only a portion of the expense can be reported that year; the rest must be spread out as an expense over several years. For more precise guidance, see *Every Landlord's Tax Deduction Guide* (see Resources in the back of this book) for how to distinguish between the two and how to report them.

- **Repairs and maintenance.** See the previous bullet on property improvement.

- **Livable property.** A phone call from a tenant in the middle of the night about their clogged toilet is probably one of the most feared scenarios that causes people to not want to deal with rentals. No one knows where this came from, but the lease usually defines what is the landlord's responsibility and what is the tenant's. The landlord has to offer a livable property (note that it falls outside the scope of this book to discuss what's livable and what's not). What's important is to make sure that, when signing the lease, the tenant understands the separation of duties. Normally, the landlord would need to take care of structural, electrical systems (the dishwasher isn't considered an electrical system in that context), pipes, and other big-ticket items. Normal maintenance of the house—including cleaning up their own... toilets—is the tenant's responsibility. Consider using the templates that come with *Every Landlord's Tax Deduction Guide*. It includes very precise language about who does what.

Guidelines

▶ **Have a good handyman in your contact list.** It's paramount to develop a great relationship with a good handyman. While I am sure you have good hands and can do most of the work yourself, this is something you would want to avoid when the number of your rental properties grows. Put simply, some work you won't be able to do or won't want to do. Having a great handyman in your contact list is a must.

▶ **Have a clear understanding of the separation of duties.** While you should have done that during the lease signature, it's worth it to have a refresher conversation from time to time. In most cases, tenants realize they haven't just checked in to a hotel where you, the landlord, are their room service. But there are times when there is a confusion. Gently remind the tenant that it is on them to fix the clogged toilet, and, if needed, point them to the specific section in the lease—or just generally say, "as we both agreed to and signed in the lease." Obviously, there are times when you will want to take care of things (since the tenant is so great and you want to please them in return), but it's a good idea to have clarity on who does what. Sometimes the tenant will call about the issue, and, after a quick chat, there is clarity between the two of you. Either ask the tenant to do a quick search online and pick the provider, or go directly to the Sears Home Services website and see what current promos they are running and pick one of them. I used Sears a few times and, in most cases, to my satisfaction. One time, though, for lubricating a stiff dial on the dishwasher, I was charged more than $200! Gosh, the synthetic oil change for my car cost me half of that! I called them, and after expressing my dissatisfaction in no uncertain terms, I was refunded a portion of the sum. Made me somewhat happy.

How-To's

HOW-TO: USE SEARS HOME SERVICES TO ORDER REPAIRS OR MAINTENANCE

To order service or repairs from Sears Home Services, follow these steps:

1. Navigate to www.searshomeservices.com.
2. Review the options available that suit your needs:

3. Review the available coupons and the ways to schedule— either via a toll-free phone number or directly online.
4. You can pick the service and then proceed to scheduling. Alternatively, you can start scheduling and then pick the service.
5. Click on "Schedule now." You should see a view similar to the following. If your HVAC needs fine tuning, then it's probably maintenance. If so, click on the "Maintenance" option:

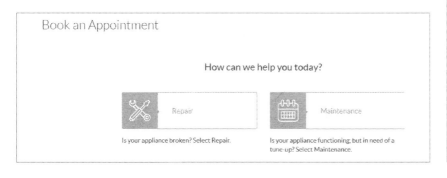

6. Click on the "Central Heating and Cooling" link.

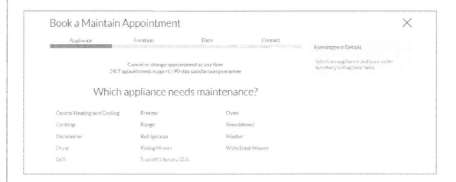

7. Click on the "Furnace" link.

8. Choose your furnace's brand; for example, Carrier:

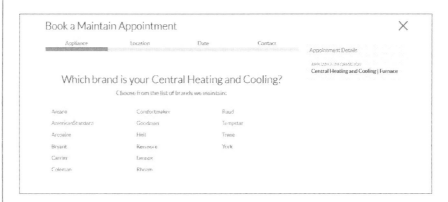

9. Let's assume there is no warranty; otherwise, you would need to call the manufacturer instead:

10. Enter your zip code where the property is located:

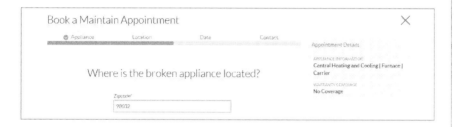

11. Pick your desired date. IMPORTANT: At this point, you can see the cost of the service on the right-hand side. Knowing the cost upfront is great so you can control the costs and, ultimately, guard your cash flow:

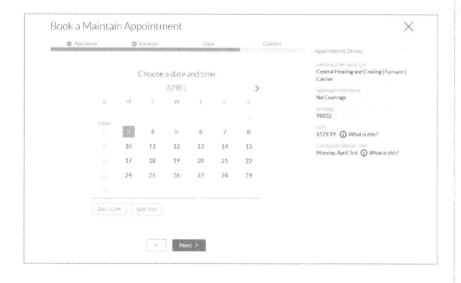

12. Finally, provide your contact information and book the service.

CHAPTER 5

Legal Entity Structure

Overview

So, how do you protect your personal assets from law suits? What legal entity structure benefits you the most from a tax-savings and legal-protection perspective? A legal entity is something else, not you personally. A legal entity has a name, phone number, address, and a bank account. It earns and spends money.

But it's not you. You own it, but you are not liable for the entity's deeds. A simple example of a legal entity is the LLC, or Limited Liability Company. A legal entity serves two key purposes: One is to shield the landlord's personal assets and the second is to offer better options to reduce your tax burden. Your legal entity structure strategy goes hand in hand with your tax strategy. A good legal entity structure will help you with the two purposes noted above—legal protection and tax liability reduction. A bad legal entity will not. This is important. In some cases, your tax liability may grow exponentially with the wrong legal entity structure, even more so than if no legal entity structure were in place. It's a loaded topic and best discussed with a professional (at least an incorporation specialist or an attorney). Be mindful of taking advice from a CPA or a bookkeeper; they are great professionals, but they have different objectives, different levels of knowledge, and different certifications.

To remind you, I am neither of these professionals, and this book is for informational purposes only. It's not advice and shouldn't be used as such. Read the books that appear in the Resources on page 147 to go deeper beyond the basics outlined in this chapter. The insights shared in this chapter were mostly sourced from these books.

If you don't have much in the way of personal assets, then you have nothing to protect. In that case, property insurance would probably be enough; maybe add some umbrella insurance on top of it, and you're good.

On the other hand, if you are like me and have accumulated substantial equity, then you should consider how to better protect it beyond insurance policies. Remember, insurance companies write their contracts in a way to limit their own liability as much as possible. If a random dude claims he slipped on your driveway (personal or rental), and you need to pay his medical bills (a total of $500K), your insurance company may well find a loophole in the contract that may get them off the hook—and get you on instead. Now you need to sell your assets—be it your home or your rentals—since they are all exposed to cover the claim.

Design

Consider the following diagram that depicts the legal entity's role and the importance of it:

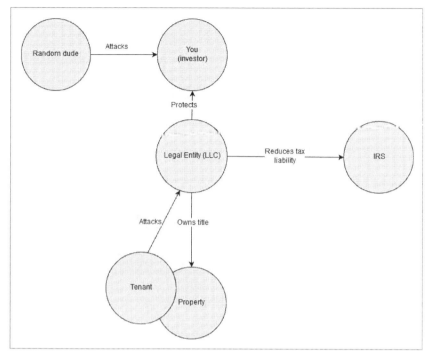

Strategy

The key objectives when setting up a legal entity are to protect your personal assets and reduce tax liability. Consider the following desires and conditions:

1. **Personal assets effectively protected from law suits.** The key objective of a legal entity is to limit your personal liability. There's a reason they call it a Limited Liability Company, or LLC, you know? There are a few rules that need to be followed to keep your legal entity in good standing, such as paying dues to the Secretary of State where the LLC was formed; keeping up with a few formalities, such as taking annual minutes notes; and a few more. If you don't maintain the entity in good standing, it may well lose its protection abilities, or, as they say in legal geek-speak, they can pierce your corporate veil. To take it further, you may want to consider whether a single-tier legal entity is sufficient or if multi-layer legal entities would be better (but that's a more advanced topic). It's best to start researching online and then schedule a meeting with an incorporation specialist or an attorney that

specializes in that area. The process of incorporation is very simple and, in most states, can be done online on the Secretary of State's website. It also can be done via incorporation specialist companies.

So, how do you decide which strategy is best for you? My approach was to first read Garret Sutton's book *Loopholes of Real Estate*, which Robert Kiyosaki recommended in his book. Apparently, Robert Kiyosaki has built a network of specialists around him, including Garret Sutton (attorney), Tom Wheelwright (CPA), and a few more. Each of them has an online presence with both freemium and premium offerings. I reached out to both and picked what's suitable for me. I decided to go with a multi-layer approach and incorporated my LLCs with Corporate Direct, a company founded by Garrett Sutton. Since then, I've been working with Cammie Warburton, senior incorporation specialist, who handles my legal entity needs. If you access their website using this affiliate link, you will be offered a $100 discount when incorporating with Corporate Direct. If you call them, consider mentioning my name; it may work too for getting $100 off. Online alternatives to Corporate Direct include LegalZoom.com and Nolo.com. Shop around.

2. **Tax liabilities reduced to the maximum extent allowed by law.** Conducting business via a legal entity not only offers better personal asset protection, but it also allows many ways to legally reduce your tax liability. Put simply, you pay less to the IRS. Tom Wheelwright writes at length on it, and I will be covering it in more depth later in the "Tax Strategy" chapter. It's worth mentioning, though, that your legal entity strategy and your tax strategy are tightly coupled and need to be well coordinated and thought through. For example, as a business owner, you could write off your meals expenses—sometimes only 50% and sometimes the full 100%—and this is fully recognized by the IRS as a legitimate business expense. There are plenty more. If you are in the top tax bracket,

spending pre-tax dollars may well be more than a 20% "discount" on your tax burden (as opposed to paying with post-tax money. That's about $20 you keep to yourself for every $100 spent on your business. You will spend much more than $100.

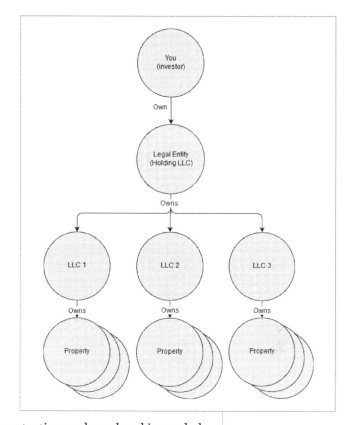

3. **Minimum overhead.** Your legal entity structure could be a simple LLC or a multi-tiered structure of LLCs and limited partnerships (LPs), and many other variations. When getting started, keeping a reasonable balance of asset protection and overhead is needed. I ended up with a two-tier entity structure, as recommended by both Garret Sutton and Tom Wheelwright in their books. In that multi-tiered structure, the top-level LLC is owned by me and my wife. Since we live in a community-property state, the LLC is considered a single-member LLC, regardless of the fact that it's owned by two of us. It's not considered a partnership by the IRS. This is important when filing taxes. A single-member LLC files taxes on Schedule C of your personal tax return (Form 1040). More on that in the "Tax Strategy" chapter. If not for a single-member LLC, I would need to file more complex tax returns, an overhead I'd rather avoid. The top-level LLC owns lower-level LLCs. Since each low-level LLC is owned by one owner (the top-level LLC), they are considered single-member LLCs as well. These low-level LLCs own actual rental properties and report their taxes on Schedule E of my personal tax return (Form 1040) since LLCs are considered a

disregarded entity. In other words, the IRS doesn't recognize them as a tax entity, thus disregarded—unless you elect them as another type of corporation... Ah, I am getting too far ahead into tax strategy! Back on track.

With the current multi-tiered approach recommended by both Garret Sutton and Tom Wheelwright in their books, I feel I have achieved a good balance of both asset protection and low overhead (when it comes to managing the business's legal entities and when filing my taxes). It also allows me to form new entities very quickly and painlessly as my business grows due to its scalable architecture.

4. **Exit strategy.** When formulating your legal entity structure, you need to assume that, at some point, you may want to wind down and retire for real—not only from the corporate world, but from actively being involved in your business. A multi-tiered approach allows this scale-down ability. This is a more advanced topic, but it ultimately needs to be addressed at some point. When passing your wealth to your children, you want to be in control of it while you are alive and reduce their tax burden when you are gone. Garret Sutton and Tom Wheelwright discuss an approach in their books that does exactly that. (See Resources, page 148.)

Concepts

▶ **Asset protection.** Assets are valuables you have—money, your car, and the equity in your home (the mortgage you pay isn't an asset). Pretty much anything of value that can be taken from you and turned into cash is an asset. You can protect personal assets by setting up a legal entity, such as an LLC, and maintain it in good standing. Bringing a lawsuit against the LLC does not mean your personal assets are exposed. Alternatively, bringing a lawsuit to you personally doesn't automatically expose your LLC's assets, such as rental property.

▸ **Community-property state.** Community-property states are where spouses are considered as one entity. This is especially important when setting up an LLC, purchasing property, or transferring title of the property between you and the LLC. The impact is mostly in taxes. For example, a married couple in a community-property state such as Washington (not Washington DC) that set up a jointly owned LLC doesn't need to file their taxes as a partnership. Instead, they can file as a single-member LLC, which simplifies the process greatly.

▸ **Corporate veil.** In legal geek-speak, a corporate veil is what gives you asset protection when you set up an LLC. If you maintain the LLC in good standing, it's hard for creditors to come after your personal assets when they attack you or your LLC and bring a lawsuit. If you don't maintain your LLC well, however, your corporate veil can be pierced via a charging order and personal assets become exposed to creditors.

▸ **Limited Liability Company (LLC).** An LLC is a type of legal entity that's designed to help you protect your assets and reduce tax liability, and it's recommended in the books I referenced earlier. (See also Resources on page 148.) Work with an incorporation specialist to discuss your situation and set up your LLC appropriately.

▸ **Registered agent.** This is the proxy of your legal entity, the LLC. Consider the following: If you move from one place to another and forget to re-route your mail, chances are an important letter, such as an invitation to court, may get lost. If you don't show up to court, you'll probably lose your case as a result. Alternatively, if you have a registered agent, the letter will be served to the registered agent's address, and they will know how to find you and notify you accordingly.

▸ **Single-member LLC.** When an LLC has one owner, it is considered a single-member LLC. For example, if you own the LLC, it's a single-member LLC. When holding a parent LLC that owns a child LLC, the parent LLC is still considered a single-member LLC. When a married couple owns an LLC in a community-property state, it's also a single-member LLC. Single-member LLCs simplify tax filing, and you don't need to use a more expensive version of TurboTax, which will be covered more in the "Tax Strategy" chapter. Single-member LLCs are of no interest to the IRS, so it calls them a disregarded entity; in other words, the IRS ignores single-member LLCs. The IRS cares about LLCs that have more than one member (called a partnership). In either case, from a legal perspective, the LLC is an entity to protect your assets, but from the IRS's perspective, the single-member LLC is non-existent, which is great—fewer hoops to jump through when filing taxes.

▶ **Sole proprietorship.** From the IRS's perspective, someone who doesn't have a legal entity and who operates as themself is the same as a single-member LLC. In both cases, it's a sole proprietorship in the eyes of the IRS. From a legal perspective, however, without a legal entity in place, there is no personal asset protection for the sole proprietor. The single-member LLC has the least friction when it comes to the IRS and asset protection. Please refer to the books mentioned earlier (see also Resources on page 148) to go deeper into it.

Guidelines

▶ **Maintain your corporate veil.** This is important. If not, your efforts with the LLC are worthless. There are prescriptive rules that explain how to do so, and they are not hard; it's all about discipline. Consult your incorporation specialist on how to protect your corporate veil, or read Garret Sutton's book for precise guidance. (See Resources, page 148).

▶ **Transfer title to the LLC.** When you purchase your rental property with lender financing, the lender will want your personal guarantee for the loan on the papers; the LLC won't do. After closure, the title of the property needs to be transferred to the LLC to take advantage of its legal asset protection. However, there may be some friction with the lender, so it's better to consult with the lender first to see if they are fine with the title transfer. Usually, the lender won't care as long as you pay the mortgage and are personally liable for it via your personal guarantee. To transfer the title, you would normally need to go through a title company. There are companies that offer this service, but they charge twice as much as the title company would (which is pretty much at-cost). The biggest cost associated with a title transfer is what the county or local authority charges that manages the records. It is important that the owners who appear on the original purchase are the same as the ones who own the LLC. For example, if you own the LLC with your spouse, it's important that the closing documents show the same. Otherwise, when transferring the title with the county, they may consider that excise tax is due (which is 2% of the property's value)—that's painful—for merely transferring the property from yourself to yourself. Don't make this mistake; consult with a title company officer; they know it best.

▶ **Use a separate address for business.** Your official business address is the one that belongs to the registered agent when you set up your LLC. The registered agent may be very far from where you live, and forwarding business mail may cost additional fees. I am renting a PO Box and use it as my business mailing address. When I move from my personal residence, I don't need to change my business address. I also would like to reduce how much I expose the address of my personal residence to the business world. Not that it's hard to find out in today's no-privacy reality.

▶ **Use a separate bank account for business transactions.** Set up separate bank accounts for each LLC you create. You will need to provide incorporation documents and a Tax ID or EIN (Employer Identification Number). These numbers will be obtained by the incorporation specialist when you first set up your LLC (for a small additional fee). Separate business bank accounts are good for maintaining the LLC in good standing and extremely helpful when managing books (more on this in the "Bookkeeping" chapter). Mixing business transactions with personal bank accounts and credit cards is a bad approach; don't do it.

▸ **Use a separate phone for business.** Use a separate line for conducting business; this is especially helpful when you have your day job. To avoid carrying two phones, I installed the Sideline iPhone app. It's free and it allows you to choose from available numbers. You can do phone calls, text, and voicemail. You can configure it to direct your calls to voicemail during the day (work hours) and then go over your messages after work. Works great for me.

How-To's

HOW-TO: DETERMINE IF YOU NEED TO SET UP AN LLC

To determine if you need to set up LLC, follow these steps.

5. Setting up an LLC makes sense in the following scenarios:
   ▸ You have accumulated equity that you'd like to protect from potential lawsuits.
   ▸ You have plans to grow your real estate business moderately.
6. Setting up a multi-layer LLC makes sense in the following scenarios:
   ▸ You have accumulated significant equity in your personal assets.
   ▸ You plan to aggressively grow your real estate business.
   ▸ Your real estate portfolio exceeds $500K, and you would like to protect each $500K of the portfolio as a separate property-owning, single-member LLC.
7. Managing your real estate investment without an LLC makes sense in the following scenarios:
   ▸ You haven't accumulated much equity.
   ▸ You don't plan to grow your real estate business.

CHAPTER 6

Bookkeeping

Overview

So, how do you manage funds to increase profitability, save on taxes, and reduce your tax liability? It all comes down to bookkeeping. This could be as simple as collecting receipts in a shoe box or as sophisticated as using a custom-built Excel spreadsheet, or using professional software such as QuickBooks yourself or jointly with your bookkeeper. It all depends on how simply your funds flow now and how complex you think they will become, and how soon.

Whatever approach you use, neatly kept books will help enormously during tax season to reduce your tax liability, and even more so should you face an IRS audit. For example, if you bought a small apartment all cash without financing, and you don't have any plans to get more rentals, then the shoe box bookkeeping method is probably your path forward. Alternatively, if you purchased a single-family home using financing, and you are planning on purchasing a few more, then QuickBooks Online and a good bookkeeper would be an approach to consider.

Design

Consider the following diagram that depicts bookkeeping and its relationship with other key components for a simple legal entity structure:

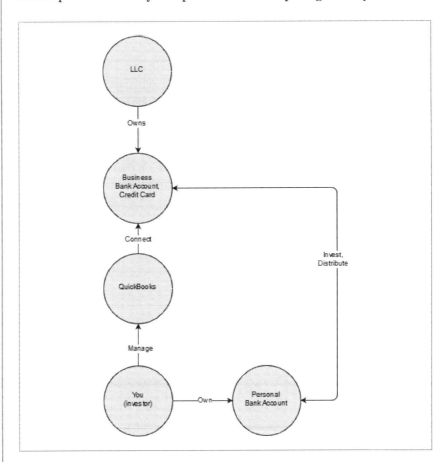

- ▶ **You (investor).** You want to keep your business records/ transactions accurate and friction free. You want to make data-driven decisions about spending nearly instantly.
- ▶ **Personal Bank Account.** You use your personal bank account to flow funds into your business account. This is considered your owner equity or investment in the business. However, in general, you don't do business expenditures from your per-

sonal account. If in the rare case you do, then you reimburse yourself from the business account. This is very similar to how you are reimbursed at your day job.

▸ **QuickBooks Online.** QuickBooks Online (QBO) is cloud software you use to manage your books. You give access to your bookkeeper if you hire one (which is highly recommended) so they can reconcile your accounts in a timely manner and help you clean up your accounting mess. QBO is connected to your business bank and business credit card accounts to pull transactions automatically, so all you need to do is categorize them in QBO (vs. punching them in manually). You use QBO to track profit and loss (P&L), the balance sheet (assets and liabilities, net worth), and to project year-end net income or loss.

▸ **Business account, credit card.** You open a separate business bank account and separate business credit card owned by the LLC. These are connected to QBO. All business expenses are managed from these accounts to maintain a clear separation between you and your legal entity. (This is mandatory but not sufficient to maintain your corporate veil, as discussed earlier in the "Legal Entity Structure" chapter).

▸ **LLC.** This is the legal entity you will manage in QBO. Transfer the property title to the LLC to take advantage of the asset protection the LLC offers. The business bank account and business credit card account are owned by the LLC, not you personally; you are the LLC's managing member, which means you manage the accounts on the LLC's behalf.

The following diagram depicts bookkeeping and its relationship with other key components when a multi-tier legal entity structure is employed. It may look scary, but it's not; it's the same simple case as discussed earlier just multiplied by three:

In addition to components outlined in the earlier diagram (bookkeeping for a simple entity structure), the following components are added for a multi-tier structure:

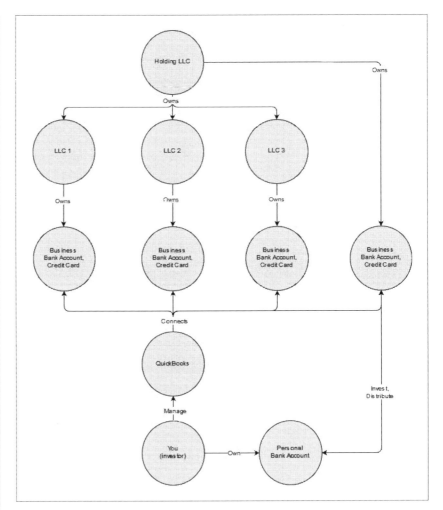

▸ **Holding LLC.** This is the holding company that provides service to the child LLCs. The holding LLC doesn't own properties; it owns child LLCs. You invest in your whole business via the holding LLC. You then transfer personal funds to the holding LLC's business account from which the holding LLC can distribute it further to its child LLCs. No funds flow between your personal account and the child LLCs' business accounts.

▸ **Holding LLC bank and credit card.** The holding LLC has it's own business bank and credit card accounts linked to QBO.

Strategy

The key objective of bookkeeping is to reduce your tax liability and reduce administrative-time waste by disciplined record keeping. Failing to do so, you risk wasting time and money, which will eventually lead to increased anxiety—not a good way to manage a business, especially if you're trying to retire early. By adopting a simple record-keeping discipline and educating yourself, you will keep more money and time to yourself. It's an excellent trade off—basic discipline for time and money, right? Consider the following desires and conditions:

1. **Clarity.** Clarity is key to achieving your bookkeeping goals (saving time and money). The trick is what to focus on. Trying to get clarity on how bookkeeping works has proven to be time and money not well spent. I gave up and hired a professional who has set up my chart of accounts (CoA), similar to the one below. But that wasn't the end of the story. A clean CoA is absolutely fundamental to successful bookkeeping, and this challenge was solved by initially hiring a professional bookkeeper. Using it effectively is another challenge, but that's exactly where the focus should be—getting the clarity of disciplined bookkeeping and sticking to a regular schedule of keeping it up. I tried to do it myself and failed miserably. After reading *QuickBooks Bookkeeping: The 10 Most Common Mistakes Everyone Makes and How to Fix Them for QuickBooks and QuickBooks Online*, I painfully yet quickly recognized myself doing all these mistakes. I reached out to the author of the book, Matt Remuzzi, and hired his team's help at CapForge. Matt and Toni at CapForge are quick to respond to my emails with precise and clear guidance and insights when I hit bookkeeping challenges—journal entries, depreciation, splits, fixed assets, debits, and credits, to mention a few. With Matt and Toni on my side, I feel confident with none of the residual anxiety I used to have before.

ACCOUNT	TYPE
Petty Cash	Bank
Business Bank Account #123	Bank
Accounts Receivable	Accounts Receivable (A/R)
My Rental Property	Fixed Assets
My Rental Property (Depreciation)	Fixed Assets
My Rental Property (Purchase)	Fixed Assets
Appliances	Fixed Assets
Appliances: Depreciation	Fixed Assets
Appliances: Original cost	Fixed Assets
Brokerage Loan (Mortgage)	Long-Term Liabilities
Intercompany Transfers	Long-Term Liabilities
Security Deposits Held	Long-Term Liabilities
Opening Balance Equity	Equity
Owner's Equity	Equity
Owner's Equity: Owner's Draw	Equity
Owner's Equity: Owner's Investment	Equity
Retained Earnings	Equity
Rent Income	Income
Business	Expenses
Business: Bank Charges	Expenses
Business: Business Development	Expenses
Business: Commissions & Fees	Expenses
Business: Dues & Subscriptions	Expenses

Business: Interest (Mortgage)	Expenses
Business: Legal & Professional Fees	Expenses
Business: Loan & Buying Fees	Expenses
Business: Meals & Entertainment	Expenses
Business: Office Supplies & Expense	Expenses
Business: Travel	Expenses
Education	Expenses
Property	Expenses
Property: Depreciation Expense	Expenses
Property: HOA Fees	Expenses
Property: Insurance	Expenses
Property: Refund (Security Deposit)	Expenses
Property: Property Improvement	Fixed Assets
Property: Repair & Maintenance	Expenses
Property: Taxes (Property)	Expenses
Uncategorized Expense	Expenses

2. **Always on.** Instant access to books is a high priority for me, especially when managing multiple companies that require multiple books. A cloud-based product with a monthly subscription model fits my needs perfectly. It's always on and available anywhere there is internet access. A monthly subscription means low monthly liabilities vs. a high upfront cost (as is usually the case with desktop-installed programs). Intuit QuickBooks Online, or QBO, was a no-brainer for me. After some trial and error, I discovered the cheapest version of the product that would work for my needs, which is QBO Simple Start.

3. **Automation and integration.** QBO connects to your business bank accounts and business credit cards (you should open business accounts—don't use personal bank accounts and credit cards; review the "Legal Entity Structure" chapter to recall why). Once connected, every transaction that happens on the business bank account or business credit card will be pulled into QBO for review and categorization, no need to type it in. Very handy. No Excel spreadsheets for me.

4. **Intuitive.** Intuitive software with clear guidance from a knowledgeable bookkeeper makes all the difference. Intuit's QBO user interface, or UI, is clean, easy, and intuitive. A clutter-free UI is only part of the story; the other part is clear guidance on how to effectively use it, which Matt and Toni at CapForge provided me with on a timely basis via emails.

5. **Minimum work during tax time.** A clean CoA and disciplined upkeep of the records makes tax season friction free (more on this in the next chapter, "Tax Strategy"). I use Intuit's product, TurboTax Online Self-Employed, to file my taxes online. That's the minimum version that allows filing Schedule C and Schedule E, which is needed when employing a multi-tier legal entity structure. If no multi-tier entity structure is in place, then a cheaper version that offers Schedule E will suffice. Although both QBO and TurboTax come from the same vendor, Intuit, there is no direct integration. TurboTax

cannot pull the information from QBO blindly. This is why it's important to structure your CoA in a way so that there is minimum work required when copy-pasting data from one to the other. The best way to do it is to study how IRS Form 1040 Schedule C and Schedule E look, and then build the CoA around it while reflecting on your business type and structure. This should greatly reduce any friction during the tax season; I can't emphasize this enough. A great bookkeeper will know how to make it so.

6. **Forward-looking projections.** Bookkeeping software like QBO is great at capturing past transactions and showing key reports, like profit and loss (P&L) and assets and liabilities. One key takeaway I took from Robert Kiyosaki and Thomas J. Stanley's books (see the Resources on page 148 in this book) is learning the finer distinctions between the various financial reports, such as the two noted above. P&L helps track net profit, which is income less expenses. This is what the IRS cares about and taxes you for—your net income as shown on the P&L. Asset and liabilities is about your wealth or net-worth growth. The IRS doesn't tax wealth. One way to increase wealth is to reduce your tax liability by increasing your expenses and/or by postponing income so that, at the end of the tax year, you show just enough net income to satisfy the IRS's criteria for not being a hobby but a legitimate business. More on this in the "Tax Strategy" chapter. It would be desirable to be able to project what your net income will look like at the end of the tax year so you can make the necessary adjustments beforehand to reduce your tax liability. For example, postpone invoices until after year end, or increase expenses this year that were already planned, such as appliance maintenance or other much-needed repairs. Matt at CapForge taught me a nice trick that's available with QBO. Here's how it works, in his own words:

   To answer your question, the easiest way to do projections I've found is to download your P&L in Excel for-

*mat for the past 4-6 months. Then you can add antici-
pated income and expenses to future months in the same
columns and accounts. As each new month goes by, you
can then compare the actuals to your projected amounts
and see how close you were. By starting with the last 4- 6
months, you can get an idea of the average trend for the
different accounts, but you don't have to keep them all as
part of your forecast. For example, once you have your
budget together, you can then just run it from Jan-Dec
for 2017.*

     *The nice thing about this also is, since you are
working in Excel, it doesn't make any changes to the
actual books!*

     Hope that helps.

     Thanks,

     Matt

My reply:

     *Matt, this is *excellent* advice! So simple yet so
effective.*

     Thank you,

     Alik

To learn more, see "How-To: Project Year-End Net Income Using
QBO and MS Excel" later in this chapter.

Concepts

▶ **Assets and liabilities.** I like Robert Kiyosaki's definition of
assets and liabilities, paraphrased as: *Assets earn you money;
liabilities take your money away.* A car is a liability (unless
you use it for making money, like Uber or Amazon delivery).
A personal residence (the home where you live) is a liability (unless you convert the equity into a HELOC that allows
you to purchase a rental property with positive cash flow). A
single-family home rental property is an asset since it earns
you money when properly planned. Your assets less liabilities

equals your net worth; the ultimate measure of wealth. Quick-Books has a report that produces an exact view of a business's assets and liabilities. Your assets should grow over time; if not, you are bleeding your wealth. For example, if you have negative cash flow, then expenses overshadow income. In that case, your numbers are broken and need to be revised. To see my overall net worth, including personal and business assets, I use another product from Intuit—Mint.com. It comes with an iOS/iPhone mobile app, which I use. It's free. The IRS doesn't care about your net worth. Well, they absolutely do care and are trying to find ways to tax it, yet unsuccessfully so far. The IRS only taxes earned or realized income, but not appreciation of a property. If you make $100K on stocks or from your day job, you are taxed. If your property appreciates $100K, you are not taxed (at least, not until you go to sell it).

▸ **Chart of accounts (CoA).** A chart of accounts is the foundation of bookkeeping. Set it up wrong, and you may end up with a higher tax liability or miss the opportunity to improve your cash flow. Just like with the foundation of a house, if it's made wrong, the whole house may cave in one day. It's the same with a CoA. Hire a good bookkeeper who's experienced with managing real estate businesses to set up your CoA. That's money very well spent.

▸ **Depreciation.** Depreciation is about losing value. Houses, cars, appliances, and home improvements depreciate over time, and the IRS allows you to deduct those losses from your gross income to reduce net income (taxable income). Put simply, depreciation is great since it helps reduce tax burden. Different assets depreciate differently and, as such, should be tracked differently so you can properly declare them when filing taxes. Tracking depreciation helps you to see how much net income to expect at the end of the fiscal year and, as such, it helps you decide how to reduce your tax burden. When filing taxes with TurboTax, it will ask different questions about depreciation instead of asking for the final number you came up with in QuickBooks, but it's usually very close or the same if tracked correctly.

▸ **Profit and loss** (**P&L**). Profit and loss is another key report (assets and liabilities was the first) that shows how much money you made or lost. The IRS cares about this one a lot. It's earned or realized income, and the IRS taxes it. This report is easily produced with QuickBooks. It should be closely tracked through the year. Also, it should be optimized to show just enough income to avoid qualifying as a hobby (which would cause you to lose the benefit of multiple business deductions). On the other hand, it should not be too high; that way, you can avoid (not evade!) paying too much in taxes. Making money as a business opens the door for such flexibility. Thomas J. Stanley puts it nicely (or was it Robert Kiyosaki?): "Cash poor, asset rich." A simple yet very memorable and effective mantra.

▸ **QBO.** QBO stands for QuickBooks Online, which is the online version of Intuit's QuickBooks software for bookkeeping. I use QBO Simple Start for each LLC I own.

Guidelines

▸ **Hire a great bookkeeper.** A great bookkeeper is the smartest and most affordable investment a real estate entrepreneur can make. It's hard work and demands attention to detail on a large scale. I'd rather research the market and work on a financing plan for a great real estate deal and let the pros do the bookkeeping. It's also the one thing that can derail the efforts of optimizing your bottom line, especially when you aspire to grow aggressively. Forget about the shoe box, the excel spreadsheets, and even managing the books yourself in QBO. I have received timely and insightful services at an excellent price that helps me prepare to grow my business, drives down my tax burden, and frees up my time so I can do the work I am best at.

▶ **Connect business bank accounts and credit cards.** Connecting bank and credit cards in QBO will enable adding transactions automatically so you won't need to do it manually. All you need to do is categorize them (and sometimes split them, to allocate an expense to more than one property). Excellent feature. Don't connect your personal bank and credit card accounts to QBO, and don't use your personal bank and credit card accounts for business expenses on a regular basis (to help you maintain your corporate veil). This was covered in the "Legal Entity Structure" chapter.

▶ **Estimate annualized income in a timely manner.** Estimating net income or loss early on allows you to foresee the impact it will have on taxes. If you anticipate losses for the holding LLC that is reported on Schedule C (discussed later in the "Tax Strategy" chapter), and those losses are being offset from the regular income reported on your W-2, then you may end up being required to file quarterly taxes—a friction that's better to avoid. To avoid paying estimated quarterly taxes, ask your employer to deduct more during the year on W-4. Here's what the IRS says about it:

Who Does Not Have to Pay Estimated Tax

If you receive salaries and wages, you can avoid having to pay estimated tax by asking your employer to withhold more tax from your earnings. To do this, file a new Form W-4 (PDF) with your employer. There is a special line on Form W-4 for you to enter the additional amount you want your employer to withhold.

You don't have to pay estimated tax for the current year if you meet **all three** *of the following conditions.*

▶ You had no tax liability for the prior year.

▶ You were a U.S. citizen or resident for the whole year.

▶ Your prior tax year covered a 12-month period.

More info:

www.irs.gov/businesses/small-businesses-self-employed/estimated-taxes

If you anticipate gains for a holding LLC that is reported on Schedule C as regular income, you may want to make some room for planned expenses that were needed anyway to help you reduce your taxable income this year. The key is to show some income to satisfy the IRS's hobby-loss rule (where the IRS may decide you are not a business since you are incurring losses over several years). In that case, the IRS can revoke your deductions. Not a good place to be. Details on how to beat the hobby-loss rule are covered in Chapter 2 in the "Deduct It!" section.

Estimating annualized and expected net income from property-holding LLCs (reported on Schedule E) is another key. This net income is considered passive income and that cannot be written off from regular income. Generally, if the property sits on a small lot of land, it will produce nice phantom losses called depreciation and should break even, if not show a loss (at best), at the end of the year. Passive losses from previous years are carried over, so if you see the property cash flows so well that the current year's depreciation cannot offset it, don't rush to spend to reduce taxable income. Instead, look for previous-year losses as additional write-offs. To learn more, see the section "How-To: Report Property Depreciation in QBO."

▶ **Issue invoices.** Issue invoices via QBO a few days before rent is due. It's easier to follow up to see who's late on rent payments, and it is easier to match the invoice with the deposit when checks are deposited, assuming the bank account is linked to QBO. Sending out invoices a few days before they are due helps renters too; it gives them a gentle reminder to write the check and also to make sure there are funds in their accounts to cover it. It helps avoid the unnecessary friction of following up and reminding them to send their checks, or dealing with bounced checks due to a lack of funds.

▶ **Map your CoA to Schedule C and Schedule E.** When building your CoA in the first place, ask your bookkeeper to create and name accounts in QBO to mimic what appears on IRS Schedule C and Schedule E as much as possible. A great bookkeeper will know how to do it. Once done, filing taxes during tax season using TurboTax will be a breeze and friction free. Print out the P&L from QBO, fill in the TurboTax fields, and mark them off on the printout. Done.

▸ **Pay with a credit or debit card.** Get a business credit and/or debit card and link it to the business account for each LLC (both child and parent). They usually come with no annual fees, so it's free. Pay business expenses with the cards so that transactions appear automatically in QBO. No petty cash and no reimbursements.

▸ **Review transactions weekly in QBO.** Log on to QBO weekly to see what transactions have been pulled from business bank and credit card accounts. For example, it could be an HOA payment that's set up for monthly bill pay, or it could be a credit card payment, an expense, a refund, rent, or any other transaction. Usually, the volume is very low. Volume grows during marketing and move-in/move-out periods naturally, but it's not as dramatic as needing to check QBO daily. A weekly log on is good enough to check in and categorize everything. It's also easier on your bookkeeper when you need to ask them something over email. (That way, you can batch all your bookkeeping questions for the week.)

▸ **Send checks via bill pay.** If a credit or debit card is not an option for a business expense, use online bill pay to send checks. They're usually free of charge and you don't need to keep your paper checkbook. No paper for me. Another even bigger benefit? It's all tracked and synced into QBO automatically.

▸ **Add electronic receipts to QBO transactions.** Every transaction in QBO must have an attachment of evidence supporting the transaction. This is a must. Most commonly, it's a receipt. A paper receipt should be either scanned or photographed using your iPhone. Email receipts should be saved as a PDF. If there's no receipt, any evidence to support the transaction must be attached. I can't stress enough how important this is. The same document can be attached to different transactions, as it may have evidence to support them. After attaching, always click on it to review the correct one was attached. I tend to attach a PDF, as it's the most common file format. Any other document can be "converted" into a PDF document file. It helps keep records neatly, which, in turn, helps with taxes down the road should any ambiguity surface later or when the IRS comes with an audit.

▸ **Comment, comment, comment.** This goes hand in hand with attaching supporting evidence for transactions, such as receipts. You can comment freely on almost anything in QBO, and you should. The more comments, the better. It helps your bookkeeper with their work, and it helps you when looking back if any ambiguity surfaces. Many transactions from business bank and credit card accounts come with their own comments, which are auto-imported into QBO. Surprisingly, they are usually useless and, in many cases, just gibberish. I usually don't delete these automatic comments; instead, I preserve them and start typing my own comments in front of them. The more comments, the better. Oh, and did I mention to comment as much as possible?

How-To's

HOW-TO: REPORT PROPERTY DEPRECIATION IN QBO

To report property depreciation in QBO, follow these steps:

1. Make sure that your CoA has an account of the Category Type "Fixed Assets" so you can capture the depreciation expense. It should look similar to the following figure. Normally, it will be a child account to the general property account. In the following example, the general account is "My Rental Property." The Category Type is "Fixed Assets," and it is set to aggregate all the fixed assets—specifically, those that depreciate over time and should be reported as such (vs. expensing them in a lump sum; the IRS wouldn't like that). (See next page.)

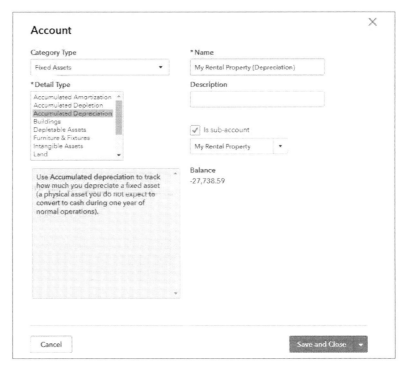

2. The child account being created is "My Rental Property (Depreciation)." Other child accounts would be "My Rental Property (Purchase)"—from the HUD statement or the final closing statement. Review the following:

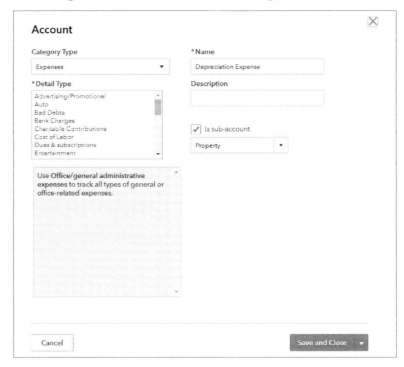

3. Make sure the CoA has a depreciation expense account. I have no idea why that's needed. I only know that modern accounting was invented several hundred years ago and hasn't changed since. It needs to have a pair of accounts—one for debits and another for credits. I just hired a bookkeeper who looks after me, end of story.

4. Calculate what can be depreciated. Land cannot be depreciated. All the rest that's part of the purchase can. Look at what's called "the HUD statement" (sometimes called "the final closing statement"), which is provided by the escrow company. Check out the bottom line and take note.

5. Look on the county or other municipality website that manages the records for this property's land value and improvement value. This is how they tax the property. Take note of the land value.

6. Subtract the land value from the bottom line on the HUD statement or the final closing statement. This is what can be depreciated. For example, if you purchased a property for $500K, and if fees to the lender, appraiser, and other good people was another $10K, then the HUD statement (or final closing statement) will show a total of $510K. If county records show the land's value was assessed at $150K for the purchase year, then what can be depreciated is $510K-$150K=$360K. This is called basis.

7. Calculate the annual depreciation. This is how much you can depreciate or claim as a valid yet phantom expense each year for the next 27.5 years, and thus pay less taxes. There are plenty of calculators online. I use this one: http://www.free-online-calculator-use.com/macrs-depreciation-calculator.html#calculator. (See graphic next page.)

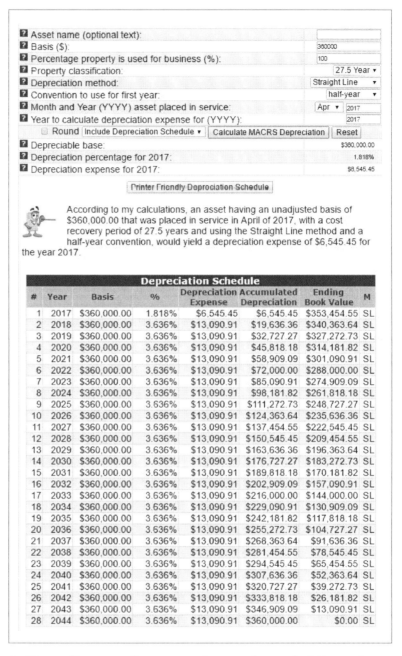

❓ Asset name (optional text):	
❓ Basis ($):	360000
❓ Percentage property is used for business (%):	100
❓ Property classification:	27.5 Year ▾
❓ Depreciation method:	Straight Line ▾
❓ Convention to use for first year:	half-year ▾
❓ Month and Year (YYYY) asset placed in service:	Apr ▾ 2017
❓ Year to calculate depreciation expense for (YYYY):	2017
☐ Round	Include Depreciation Schedule ▾	Calculate MACRS Depreciation	Reset
❓ Depreciable base:	$360,000.00
❓ Depreciation percentage for 2017:	1.818%
❓ Depreciation expense for 2017:	$6,545.45

Printer Friendly Depreciation Schedule

According to my calculations, an asset having an unadjusted basis of $360,000.00 that was placed in service in April of 2017, with a cost recovery period of 27.5 years and using the Straight Line method and a half-year convention, would yield a depreciation expense of $6,545.45 for the year 2017.

Depreciation Schedule

#	Year	Basis	%	Depreciation Expense	Accumulated Depreciation	Ending Book Value	M
1	2017	$360,000.00	1.818%	$6,545.45	$6,545.45	$353,454.55	SL
2	2018	$360,000.00	3.636%	$13,090.91	$19,636.36	$340,363.64	SL
3	2019	$360,000.00	3.636%	$13,090.91	$32,727.27	$327,272.73	SL
4	2020	$360,000.00	3.636%	$13,090.91	$45,818.18	$314,181.82	SL
5	2021	$360,000.00	3.636%	$13,090.91	$58,909.09	$301,090.91	SL
6	2022	$360,000.00	3.636%	$13,090.91	$72,000.00	$288,000.00	SL
7	2023	$360,000.00	3.636%	$13,090.91	$85,090.91	$274,909.09	SL
8	2024	$360,000.00	3.636%	$13,090.91	$98,181.82	$261,818.18	SL
9	2025	$360,000.00	3.636%	$13,090.91	$111,272.73	$248,727.27	SL
10	2026	$360,000.00	3.636%	$13,090.91	$124,363.64	$235,636.36	SL
11	2027	$360,000.00	3.636%	$13,090.91	$137,454.55	$222,545.45	SL
12	2028	$360,000.00	3.636%	$13,090.91	$150,545.45	$209,454.55	SL
13	2029	$360,000.00	3.636%	$13,090.91	$163,636.36	$196,363.64	SL
14	2030	$360,000.00	3.636%	$13,090.91	$176,727.27	$183,272.73	SL
15	2031	$360,000.00	3.636%	$13,090.91	$189,818.18	$170,181.82	SL
16	2032	$360,000.00	3.636%	$13,090.91	$202,909.09	$157,090.91	SL
17	2033	$360,000.00	3.636%	$13,090.91	$216,000.00	$144,000.00	SL
18	2034	$360,000.00	3.636%	$13,090.91	$229,090.91	$130,909.09	SL
19	2035	$360,000.00	3.636%	$13,090.91	$242,181.82	$117,818.18	SL
20	2036	$360,000.00	3.636%	$13,090.91	$255,272.73	$104,727.27	SL
21	2037	$360,000.00	3.636%	$13,090.91	$268,363.64	$91,636.36	SL
22	2038	$360,000.00	3.636%	$13,090.91	$281,454.55	$78,545.45	SL
23	2039	$360,000.00	3.636%	$13,090.91	$294,545.45	$65,454.55	SL
24	2040	$360,000.00	3.636%	$13,090.91	$307,636.36	$52,363.64	SL
25	2041	$360,000.00	3.636%	$13,090.91	$320,727.27	$39,272.73	SL
26	2042	$360,000.00	3.636%	$13,090.91	$333,818.18	$26,181.82	SL
27	2043	$360,000.00	3.636%	$13,090.91	$346,909.09	$13,090.91	SL
28	2044	$360,000.00	3.636%	$13,090.91	$360,000.00	$0.00	SL

8. Depending on a few parameters, such as what time of year the property was purchased, you will be given a number to use as your annual depreciation expense. Use the straight line depreciation method (other methods are beyond the scope of this discussion). For example, it may look like the following:

9. The numbers in the "Depreciation Expense" column are what you would punch into QBO when recording depreciation,

as shown in the previous figure. Notice how after 27.5 years in service, the property lost value from the IRS's perspective—regardless of the fact it appreciated four times or more! When filing taxes during the tax season, TurboTax will ask a few simple questions and will get to the same number. There is no way to punch this number directly into TurboTax. It's important, though, to track it here in QBO, as discussed previously in the "Guidelines" section.

10. To record depreciation, add a journal entry by clicking on the ✕ icon:

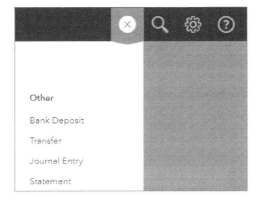

11. Click on the "Journal Entry" link.

12. Add two line items to the journal entry. One is a credit for the fixed-asset account "My Rental Property (Depreciation)" and the other is a debit for "Property: Depreciation Expense." Make sure the journal date is set for the end of the tax year (in this case, 12/31/16), as shown in the following figure:

13. Check your work by running a profit-and-loss report for the entire year. Depreciation expenses should be similar to what's shown in the following figure. (Note: The numbers don't match, as there are additional depreciation expenses besides property depreciation):

▼ Property	0.00
Depreciation Expense	11,156.39
HOA Fees	1,800.00
Insurance	957.02
Repair & Maintenance	218.88
Taxes (Property)	2,583.82

HOW-TO: REPORT MORTGAGE INTEREST PAID AS AN EXPENSE IN QBO

If you want to report the mortgage interest you paid as an expense, here are the prerequisites:

- ▶ Mortgage payments must be automatically withdrawn from the business account for a property. This is usually done on the lender's website where you can schedule automatic withdrawals from the business bank account on a monthly basis. The withdrawals are usually a lump sum of principal, interest, and escrow (escrow will cover insurance and property taxes if you set it up that way). I usually don't set up escrow unless there are significant benefits to doing so. I pay taxes and insurance separately myself. Less dependency and much cleaner operations.
- ▶ A business account must be connected in QBO. In QBO, the mortgage payment will appear as a lump sum that either needs to be split (into 12 monthly payments) or reported in full at the end of the year when the bank sends Form 1098, as required by law. Form 1098 is where the bank reports how much interest you paid that tax year. So, instead of doing splits each month, I'd rather do it once after getting Form 1098 right after year end for the tax season.
- ▶ Mortgage interest is reported as a journal entry in QBO.

To report mortgage interest paid as an expense in QBO, follow these steps:

1. Make sure that your CoA has an account for the Category Type "Long Term Liabilities" to track the mortgage. It should look similar to the following:

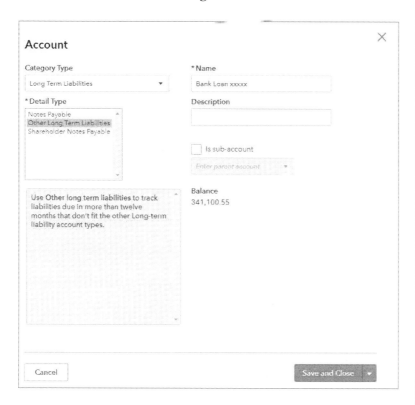

2. Make sure your CoA has an account of the Category Type "Expenses" to capture the mortgage interest paid as an expense. It should look similar to the graphic at the top of the next page.

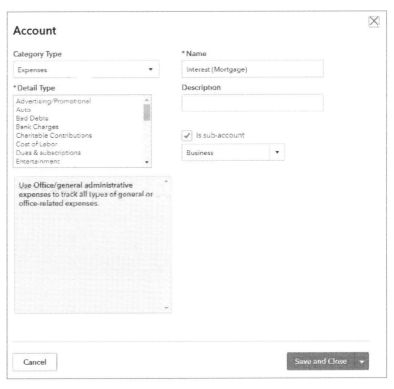

3. If the journal entry already exists and needs updating, find the existing one by clicking on the search icon at the top; it appears as a magnifying glass:

4. Click on the "Advanced Search" link. You should see the following:

5. Make sure "Journal Entries" is selected from the drop-down list and click on the "Search" button.

6. From the resulting list, select the desired journal entry and update it with the value of interest paid that appears on Form 1098 that the lender sent. It should appear in Box 1 of the form.

7. If the journal entry doesn't exist yet and you need to create a new one, click on the plus icon; you should see a view similar to the following:

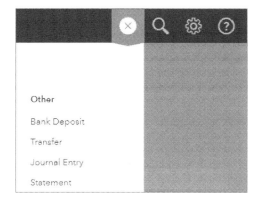

8. Click on the "Journal Entry" link.

9. Add two line items to the journal entry. One is a credit for the long-term liability account representing the loan and the other is a debit for the expense account representing the interest paid. Make sure the journal date is set for the end of the tax year (in this case, 12/21/16), as shown in the following figure:

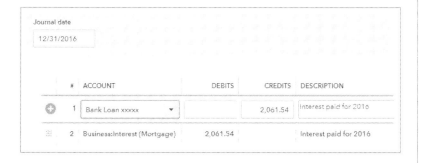

10. Click the "Save" or "Save and Close" button.

11. Check to ensure the mortgage interest expense is properly recorded in the profit-and-loss report, and make sure to use the current year (i.e. "This Year") for the reporting date range to capture it correctly. It should look similar to the following:

HOW-TO: PROJECT YEAR-END NET INCOME USING QBO AND MS EXCEL

To project year-end net income using QBO and MS Excel, follow these steps:

1. In QBO, click on "Reports" in the navigation sidebar.
2. Click on the "Run" link under the "Profit and Loss" section.
3. Change "Report period" to "This year."
4. Change "Display columns by" to "Months."
5. Click on the "Run report" button.
6. Click on the "Export to Excel" option on the upper-right side of the report:

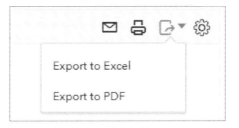

7. The report will download as an Excel file. Open it in Excel and review it. Not all of the values may show.
8. In Excel, click on the "Enable editing" button to make the values appear. It should look similar to the following:

	Jan 2017	Feb 2017	Mar 2017	Apr 2017	May 2017	Jun 2017	Jul 2017	Aug 2017	Sep 2017	Oct 2017	Nov 2017	Dec 2017	Total
My Company, LLC													
Profit and Loss													
January - December 2017													
Income													
Rent Income	2,295.00	2,295.00	918.00	0.00	0.00	0.00	0.00	0.00	0.00	0.00	0.00	0.00	5,508.00
Total Income	$2,295.00	$2,295.00	$918.00	$0.00	$0.00	$0.00	$0.00	$0.00	$0.00	$0.00	$0.00	$0.00	$5,508.00
Gross Profit	$2,295.00	$2,295.00	$918.00	$0.00	$0.00	$0.00	$0.00	$0.00	$0.00	$0.00	$0.00	$0.00	$5,508.00
Expenses													
Business	0.00	0.00	0.00	0.00	0.00	0.00	0.00	0.00	0.00	0.00	0.00	0.00	0.00
Bank Charges	0.00	0.00	15.00	5.00	0.00	0.00	0.00	0.00	0.00	0.00	0.00	0.00	20.00
Interest (Mortgage)	262.37	1,155.28	1,153.60	0.00	0.00	0.00	0.00	0.00	0.00	0.00	0.00	6,000.00	8,571.25
Legal & Professional Fees	0.00	250.00	0.00	0.00	0.00	0.00	0.00	0.00	0.00	0.00	0.00	0.00	250.00
Total Business	$262.37	$1,405.28	$1,168.60	$5.00	$0.00	$0.00	$0.00	$0.00	$0.00	$0.00	$0.00	$6,000.00	$8,841.25
Property	0.00	0.00	0.00	0.00	0.00	0.00	0.00	0.00	0.00	0.00	0.00	0.00	0.00
Depreciation Expense	0.00	0.00	0.00	0.00	0.00	0.00	0.00	0.00	0.00	0.00	0.00	17,069.90	17,069.90
Documents, Certs & Filings	0.00	0.00	275.00	0.00	0.00	0.00	0.00	0.00	0.00	0.00	0.00	0.00	275.00
HOA Fees	200.00	200.00	100.00	0.00	0.00	0.00	0.00	0.00	0.00	0.00	0.00	0.00	500.00
Taxes (Property)	0.00	0.00	188.47	0.00	0.00	0.00	0.00	0.00	0.00	0.00	0.00	0.00	188.47
Total Property	$200.00	$200.00	$563.47	$0.00	$0.00	$0.00	$0.00	$0.00	$0.00	$0.00	$0.00	$17,069.90	$18,033.37
Total Expenses	$462.37	$1,605.28	$1,732.07	$5.00	$0.00	$0.00	$0.00	$0.00	$0.00	$0.00	$0.00	$23,069.90	$26,874.62
Net Operating Income	$1,832.63	$689.72	-$814.07	-$5.00	$0.00	$0.00	$0.00	$0.00	$0.00	$0.00	$0.00	-$23,069.90	-$21,366.62
Net Income	$1,832.63	$689.72	-$814.07	-$5.00	$0.00	$0.00	$0.00	$0.00	$0.00	$0.00	$0.00	-$23,069.90	-$21,366.62

9. Play with the numbers while observing the "Total Net Income" cell. (In the figure above, this is the last cell on the far right on line 24.) Ideally, it is at or below zero due to depreciation offsetting the gross profit, along with other expenses. That's true for the property-holding child LLC, which is reported on Schedule E as passive income.

10. For the parent (or holding) LLC, which reports regular income on Schedule C, it should show positive income—just enough to avoid the hobby-loss rule. You want to ensure the IRS categorizes you as a business to avoid losing your business deductions.

CHAPTER 7

Tax Strategy

Overview

Tax is the biggest expense you'll have. So, what's the optimal tax strategy, and how do we execute it to drive down our tax burden legally? You are taxed on net income, which is gross income less expenses and deductions. You are not taxed on your wealth or net worth. Depending on your goals—whether that's focusing on cash now or growing your wealth—your tax strategy will vary. To reduce your tax liability, you would either need to reduce your net income or increase your expenses. This chapter on tax strategy is about getting you prepared to confidently face tax season. It will help you to anticipate, plan, and execute a strategy that will result in low to zero tax burden on the one hand while also showing a reasonable level of income to avoid unnecessary IRS interest in your business.

Design

Assuming that a multi-tiered legal entity structure is employed (as described earlier in this book), the following diagram depicts the key components of the tax strategy and its relationships:

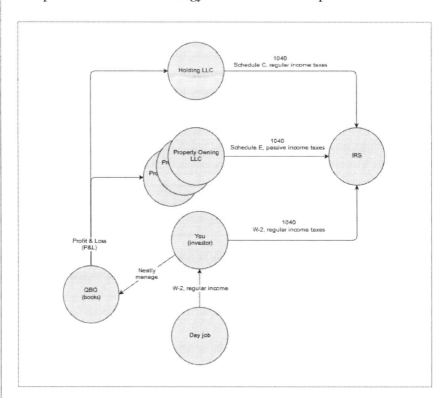

▸ **Holding LLC.** The holding LLC is the legal entity that you own directly. It doesn't own any property, it owns child LLCs. The holding LLC provides management services to the child LLCs, and any income generated by the holding LLC is considered earned/regular income. The holding LLC reports this income on Schedule C of Form 1040, and losses can be written off from day-job income. Tax deductions for business use of your home (keeping a home office) and mileage for business use of your car also go on Schedule C. The holding LLC is considered a single-member LLC when it's owned by both spouses in a community-property state such as Washington, and the IRS considers it a sole proprietorship.

▸ **Property-owning LLC.** Property-owning LLCs are owned

by the holding LLC and not directly by you. They are all single-member LLCs owned by the holding LLC (also a single-member LLC), so there's no need to report this income as a partnership; instead, it's reported on your personal tax returns on Form 1040. Property-owning LLCs own investment properties directly and own the title on the properties. They are involved in generating passive income and, as such, you report this income on Schedule E of Form 1040. Passive losses cannot be written off from regular income, but they can be carried over year after year, helping you to offset other passive income.

▸ **IRS.** Uncle Sam wants your money. But on a serious note, the IRS created more than 70,000 pages of tax code loopholes so you could take advantage of them and keep more money to yourself. In fact, the IRS wants you to keep more of your money as long as you do what they want you to do (for example, investing in real estate).

▸ **You** (**investor**). You want to pay less in taxes and keep more money to yourself.

▸ **Day job.** This is your 9-to-5 office or cubicle job. You are paid twice a month, and the paystub shows federal tax withholding—your income tax. Your day job is great for helping you qualify for loans, so don't quit it yet (or don't let them lay you off). Your annual income is reported to you by your company on Form W-2. The income reported on your W-2 is then entered into TurboTax when it's time to file. It's considered regular or earned income, taxed at pre-defined rates as defined by the IRS's progressive tax brackets. There's not much in the way of deductions here, if any. You use your day job to sustain your lifestyle and to show lenders you are credit worthy.

▸ **QBO** (**books**). QBO or QuickBooks Online is a cloud-based service coming from Intuit, the same company that offers TurboTax (I use it) and Mint.com (which is free, and I use it as well to quickly see my overall net worth). QBO is used to track business transactions—expenses and income—and helps you to project year-end profit and loss so you can adjust your expenditures accordingly, optimizing around taxes. QBO manages the holding company that's reported on Schedule C of Form 1040, and it also manages the property-owning child LLCs that are reported on Schedule E of Form 1040.

Strategy

The key objective of formulating a tax strategy is to keep more money to yourself by reducing your tax liabilities, both for the short and long term. Consider the following desires and conditions as supporting principles of this objective:

- ▶ **Increase passive losses.** This is smart whether your income is passive or ordinary. For example, your day job is ordinary income, while the rental income you earn from rental properties is passive income. It's important to distinguish between the two because when passive income shows a profit (this is when rent is higher than the total monthly liabilities, such as loan interest, insurance, and taxes), it's taxed on top of your day-job income. This means if you are in the top tax bracket, you are taxed for both to the fullest. For example, if your W-2 shows annual income of $130K and your rental net income is $10K, you are taxed at the tax bracket for your combined income ($140K). However, the opposite is not true. For example, if your W-2 shows earnings of $130K and your rental net income shows a loss of $10K, you are still taxed for the W-2's $130K—not the $120K ($130K-$10K). This is because the $10K loss is from passive income. "Then why worry about passive losses at all?" you may be asking. The good thing about passive losses is that they can be carried over year after year to help offset your passive income when it shows a profit. For example, in 2016, let's say you had $10K in passive losses on rental property (you don't pay additional taxes, as you only pay taxes on realized income). Then, in

2017, let's say you made $12K in net passive income on rental property—great! The passive loss of $10K from 2016 is carried over to the next year, helping to offset the $12K in passive income gained in 2017. The $12K in passive income minus the $10K in passive losses equals a total of $2K in net passive income in 2017. You pay $0 taxes in 2016 due to the losses, and you only pay taxes on $2K in 2017, which is probably around $400 depending on your tax bracket. You don't pay taxes on the entire $12K in 2017, which would have been around $2.4K. So, by carrying over passive losses from 2016 to 2017, you saved $2K in taxes. The magic part about the passive losses is that the majority of them come from a phantom expense called depreciation.

▶ **Depreciation only applies to the structure or building (the house itself), not the land it sits on.** In that case, a townhouse is the ideal property to "lose" money on since it doesn't have much land, so the majority of the purchase is the structure itself, which is eligible for depreciation. I am not a fan of townhomes for other reasons, as described in detail in the "Target Niche" chapter. But from a depreciation perspective, condos or townhomes are great loss-generators. Imagine a portfolio of large-lot houses that lose less on depreciation (bummer) compared to a townhome or two, which are great for depreciation losses, and since all of them are passive losses, they can and should offset one's passive income. The bottom line? Less realized income and less paid in taxes.

▶ **Keep money in the business.** Your day job should take care of your daily cash needs and cost of living. Keep it, don't quit. Another big reason to keep your day job is to score better terms when financing, as outlined earlier in the "Guidelines" section within "Financing." With that said, keep business profits in the business for further investments. The IRS allows business profits to be reinvested back into the business as a down payment for purchasing another investment property in pre-tax dollars. A layered, multi-tier legal entity structure and corresponding bookkeeping structure helps keep the funds flowing between the entities without showing on your personal bank account. There's nothing shady here; in fact, it's a good practice to avoid intermingling personal and business funds, and it reduces the friction in managing your funds while also avoiding any tears in your corporate veil. Finally, when applying for financing that is personally guaranteed (I am yet to get to the point where lenders lend me money as a business), the lender will ask to see your personal financial statements. If large sums of money appear to be going in and out of your personal accounts, the lender will ask you to explain why.

▸ **Reduce regular income.** I still haven't figured this out completely, but the idea is this: Be cash poor and asset rich. You are not taxed on assets, wealth, or net worth. You are taxed on realized income. Growing your net worth doesn't "linearly" increase your tax burden. However, increasing your regular income does, as it's based on the relevant tax brackets. If I grow my net worth mostly through passive income (as opposed to regular income or capital gains), that's the sweet spot.

▸ **Streamline tax filing.** This is a key design principle for me. TurboTax should be able to handle my situation friction free. If I need to hire a tax specialist to file my taxes, then I am doing something wrong—or something very creative, aggressive, or complex. This day will come, but not today. Today, TurboTax should do. Alternatively, there is nothing wrong with hiring a good and knowledgeable CPA for a tax strategy consultation. You can also learn a lot by reading the Q&A on certain forums (more on that in the "Continuing Education" chapter later in this book). And finally, you can educate yourself by reading great books (see the Resources on page 148). That said, filing taxes is tedious work that should be done through software. So, TurboTax Online it is!

▸ **Take advantage of key business deductions.** If taxes are the largest expense you'll face, then the first thing you need to look at are the key deductions that'll help you reduce your tax liability. Depreciation is arguably the largest (and most painless) deduction, as it doesn't require you to spend money besides the property purchase itself. Be mindful of depreciation recapture, however. Business use of your home and car are additional straightforward deductions that are easily done in TurboTax. I expense these on the holding LLC—the LLC that owns the property-owning child LLCs but doesn't hold any properties itself. This makes sense since the holding LLC's purpose is to do the overall management of child LLCs, research, and driving around. Just be sure to pay close attention to your office and car deductions. If they are not tracked in QBO and not taken into account when projecting year-end net income, you run the risk of showing too little income and qualifying as a hobby—or worse, you may end up with tax liabilities. This could result in needing to pay quarterly estimated taxes the following year. To learn more, see "How-To: Project Year-End Net Income Using QBO and MS Excel" in the "Bookkeeping" chapter.

▸ **Take advantage of lower tax brackets.** In addition to reducing regular income and keeping funds in the business, you can shift income to lower tax brackets by employing your family. Cleaning the office or the property before move in, painting, electronic record keeping—anything a kid can do, he or she should do. Commissions only, no allowances allowed. The beauty is that, for a business, it's a legitimate expense, driving down your net income; but for a kid, it's tax free since it's unlikely they'll earn more than the standard deduction, which was $6,300 in 2016. So, your kid worked legitimately for you in 2016 and was paid up to $6,300; you write it off as a legitimate business expense and save around $1,500 that you would have paid in taxes if you'd kept the money and hadn't employed your kid. Worse, you would have given the kid that money as allowance anyway, losing on taxes and missing the opportunity to educate your offspring on how the world works outside of their mobile phone. Lower tax brackets also work when partnering with parents who've retired, but I haven't tested it.

Concepts

▸ **1099.** This is an IRS form that you, as an employer, need to issue—usually by the end of January—to those who are sole proprietors (unincorporated) if you paid them more than $600 annually. This may change based on IRS guidelines. For example, I employed an architect who's doing business as a sole proprietor and isn't incorporated in any way, so I needed to issue a 1099 for him. He has done an outstanding job at an excellent price. I hired him twice and will hire him again. Others who operate as an LLC or Inc. (or other type of corporation) do not require you to issue a 1099. Don't issue a 1099 to your kid when employing them since they would need to pay sole proprietor taxes if you do this. I made this mistake and needed to correct it so my daughter could keep more of the money to herself. Instead, issue a W-2, which doesn't require your kid to pay employment taxes if their net income doesn't exceed the standard deduction. Also, you don't need to pay employment taxes for a child under 18. I use https://www.track1099.com/ to issue both 1099s and W-2s. For $3.99 a piece, the website sends the forms to me, to the employee, and then electronically to the IRS. Very cool.

▸ **Employment tax.** Employment tax is Social Security and Medicare (FICA). When employing your children who are under 18, there's no need to withhold and pay these taxes. Things change, though, if your business partner is anyone other than your spouse.

▸ **Passive income losses.** Income from rental properties is considered passive income. It can turn profitable when the annual total rent income overshadows the annual total expenses, including phantom expenses such as depreciation. Passive income can become passive losses when expenses overshadow the gross income. This is important since passive income losses cannot always be written off regular or earned W-2 income. (Sometimes it can, as well see a couple sentences below.) Passive income losses are actually a good thing when they're the result of depreciation or when they're deductions for the business use of your home or car, as these aren't real hard expenses; you don't actually spend real dollars. Passive income losses don't go to waste; instead, they can be carried over to the next year. In 2016, I had a little over $21,000 in passive losses. I claimed these to offset my taxable passive income in 2017. If my MAGI (modified adjusted gross income) were below $100K (it's not—remember, I am in the software industry in the Greater Seattle Area), I could write off the passive income losses from my regular income (up to $25K), and then gradually (not the full loss amount) from MAGI below $150K. After that, no passive losses can be written off from regular income and instead need to be written off from passive income from other passive activity. I have a few properties; some show passive losses and some show profit. The passive losses offset the passive profit, and I don't need to pay taxes as a result. I do need to pay taxes on my day-job income, however. TurboTax Online does a great job of capturing it all and calculating what I owe to the IRS, or what the IRS owes to me. In 2016, it was the latter.

▶ **Depreciation recapture.** If depreciation is magic, then depreciation recapture is a curse. What I can tell from reading in books and online is there's no escape from it. Depreciation recapture is when you are taxed 25% of what you have claimed in depreciation over the years when you sell your rental property. If you sell the property at a price higher than the purchase price, then this is considered a capital gain, and it's taxed at 15%, as any other capital gain would be. (This is assuming you held the property for more than a year. If you held it for a shorter period, chances are it would be taxed as regular income at your tax bracket, and if you're a high-income earner, then a higher tax bracket applies.) The good news is that capital gains can be offset by passive losses carried over from previous years. You can't do this with depreciation recapture, however; that's probably why the strategy is called buy and hold (forever), so you never have to deal with depreciation recapture. Another path forward is using a 1031 exchange, which I haven't tried yet. This is where taxes may be deferred forever, but this is outside the scope of this book. I have just offloaded a property that appreciated 16% year over year (YoY) and produced a 25% gain cash on cash (CoC). While all is good, I bit it with depreciation recapture when filing my 2017 taxes. I have exact numbers in my article here: 4 Ways Investing In Rental Homes Grows My Net Worth (plus Bonus #5, minus Caution #6). Note: Claiming depreciation is mandatory. You cannot avoid depreciation recapture by not claiming the depreciation deduction. Not claiming depreciation wouldn't be smart in my view anyway.

▸ **Hobby loss rule.** While generally it's a good idea to legitimately show as little income as possible by utilizing different tax deductions, there is a limit to the extent you can manage a business and lose money. The IRS may come in and say, "You aren't a business at all. You are just trying to take advantage of business deductions but never meant to make money. You are a hobby, and, as such, you aren't eligible to those business deductions. Pay it all back." Ouch! Generally, this would be applicable to the holding LLC, which is reported on Schedule C and considered regular income. Rental income is considered passive income, and it is reported on Schedule E. The IRS doesn't care about the child LLC that holds the property—or, more precisely, disregards it—so this LLC is called a disregarded entity. For the holding LLC, there are two tests that need to be met to avoid the hobby loss rule: the profit test and the behavior test. The profit test shows there was a profit for any three years within the last five years. If this test isn't met, the behavior test should show that you acted as a business with the intent to make money. For more on this, see the book called *Deduct It!: Lower Your Small Business Taxes* (listed in the Resources on page 148 in this book). In Chapter 2, it discusses in detail how to pass the behavior test. I am sticking with the profit test so I never have to bother with this one.

▶ **Itemized deduction.** This type of deduction is applicable to personal taxes (but not business taxes). The opposite approach is the standard deduction. The itemized deduction is where you claim (itemize) different personal deductions, such as tuition, childcare, HELOC interest paid, personal residence mortgage interest paid, etc. TurboTax will advise you which one to take, but if all of your itemized deductions don't exceed the standard deduction, then you should consider taking the standard deduction, and this is what TurboTax will recommend. In 2016, the standard deduction was $6,300, and for a married couple, we could claim $12,600 in standard deductions. So that's what we did, as it was more than our itemized deductions. TurboTax was great to call it out. In 2017, I used the itemized deduction, as my personal residence property taxes were around $10K; also, my daughter goes to university (tuition expenses), and my HELOC was well above $100K all year round (the maximum I could claim in interest paid for it). Oh wait… they are considering increasing the standard deduction to $30K? Whoa!

▶ **Quarterly estimated tax.** Businesses may need to pay quarterly estimated taxes. That's a pain in the butt I would rather avoid. With your day job, the tax is withheld on each paycheck, so, effectively, you pay taxes twice a month, and then you file taxes annually to recalculate it all again for a refund. For businesses, it's quarterly, and you need to estimate what it could be and then pay it. There are easy ways to avoid paying quarterly estimated taxes, as guided by the IRS. See the "Guidelines" section below for details.

▶ **Ordinary income.** This is your day-job income reported on your W-2, also called earned income. This is taxed at your current tax bracket. Income from the holding LLC that does active business managing your child LLCs (the ones that own the properties) is also considered ordinary income. You cannot write off your LLC's business expenses from your W-2 income; however, you can claim business deductions from your business income (reported on Schedule C). You cannot claim passive losses on ordinary income unless you make less than $100K (MAGI), and you can only write off up to $25K in passive losses, which gradually get lower and are disallowed once you pass $150K (MAGI).

▸ **Passive income.** Passive income comes from things like rental properties. Passive income can be offset by passive losses. Passive income is taxed just like any other income according to your tax bracket.

▸ **Tax credit.** A tax credit is when your tax is reduced dollar for dollar. For example, if you buy a Tesla (not a fan of the Tesla, it's just a catchy example), you get a federal tax credit of $7,500. So, if TurboTax showed that you owe Uncle Sam $7,500 in taxes but you bought a Tesla that year, chances are TurboTax will show you owe $0 after you punch it in. Considering an effective tax rate of 20%, $7,500 in tax credits is close to $40K in tax deductions. (See the next bullet for a full explanation.)

▸ **Tax deduction.** A tax deduction reduces taxable income. For example, if your taxes are based on regular income of $100K, then a deduction of $40K (geez, wouldn't it be cool?!) will make TurboTax calculate taxes on $60K. To continue the example, if the effective tax rate is 20%, your taxes would be $20K on $100K, while "only" $12.5K on $60K. Using a tax deduction of $40K would save you $7,500 (money not paid to Uncle Sam). Geez, this $40K deduction is like buying a Tesla... for the mere list price of $80K.

▸ **W-2.** This is the annual form your company sends you showing how much you made and how much taxes you paid.

▸ **W-4.** This form is used to ask your employer to increase your tax withholding. Ugh... what? Why would I want to do that? Well, I used to do this to bring less money home so I would have less to spend during the year, and then I'd gladly get a fat tax refund the next year. In a way, it helped me. Then I decided it's unwise, and I have discipline now using www. Mint.com to control my personal budget. What a W-4 is good for is to withhold additional taxes so that, at the year end, you show no tax liability. Otherwise, you will need to file and pay estimated quarterly taxes; something that's an administrative friction I'd rather avoid. See "How-To: Project Year-End Net Income Using QBO and MS Excel" in the "Bookkeeping" chapter to estimate whether your holding LLC will show a loss or a profit. If it's a loss, consider withholding more taxes during the year by filling out a W-4 to avoid quarterly estimated taxes.

▶ **Standard deduction.** Every year, the IRS publishes how much everyone gets to deduct; this is the standard deduction. In 2016, it was $6,300 and double for a married couple. I took the standard deduction since my itemized deduction didn't beat the standard deduction (for a married couple filing a joint return). TurboTax did a great job figuring it all out for me. This year, I'm sure I will be using the standard deduction again unless the IRS jacks it up to $10K. There's even been talk of them jacking it up to $30K!? I am all for that.

Guidelines

▶ **Anticipate.** Model what the business's net income would be at year end. To learn how to do this, see "How-To: Project Year-End Net Income Using QBO and MS Excel" in the "Bookkeeping" chapter. Optimize for passive losses coming from the property-owning child LLCs. Depreciation is something that's known long beforehand; taxes and mortgage interest are known as well. Play with your rental income and try to estimate any potential additional expenses that could be applied this year—for example, fixing, upgrading, painting, etc. Keep in mind, these improvements should be depreciated on your tax return as opposed to expensed as a lump sum. That said, any repairs or maintenance could be expensed as a lump sum. Optimize the holding LLC's net income to show some profit.

▸ **Employ your family.** No more allowance money for the kids. Paying family to work in your business is a common practice that shifts some of the business's income to lower tax brackets, helping you to save big on taxes. The work should be legitimate, such as office cleaning and electronic record keeping, and so on. The wage should be reasonable too and comparable to the market. Kids would love it!

▸ **Establish a legal entity.** You'll want to establish a legal entity, such as an LLC, to protect your business. This was discussed at length in the "Legal Entity Structure" chapter, and the emphasis there was on personal asset protection. Here the emphasis is on the business deductions that come with creating an LLC.

▸ **Keep the books neat.** I can't stress this enough. If you desire to grow your business and quickly, then hire a good bookkeeper. They will pay for themselves many times over. Neat books make planning, assessment, and filing taxes a breeze. To learn more on this topic, see the "Bookkeeping" chapter.

▸ **Avoid quarterly estimated taxes.** To estimate year-end net income, see "How-To: Project Year-End Net Income Using QBO and MS Excel" in the "Bookkeeping" chapter. If you're anticipating losses with the holding LLC, consider withholding more taxes from your day job by filing a new Form W-4 with your employer. If there are no tax liabilities at year end, there's no need to pay quarterly estimated taxes. Here it is in the IRS's own words:

Who Does Not Have to Pay Estimated Tax

If you receive salaries and wages, you can avoid having to pay estimated tax by asking your employer to withhold more tax from your earnings. To do this, file a new Form W-4 (PDF) with your employer. There is a special line on Form W-4 for you to enter the additional amount you want your employer to withhold.

You don't have to pay estimated tax for the current year if you meet **all three** *of the following conditions.*

- ▸ You had no tax liability for the prior year.
- ▸ You were a U.S. citizen or resident for the whole year.
- ▸ Your prior tax year covered a 12-month period.

More info:

www.irs.gov/businesses/small-businesses-self-employed/estimated-taxes

- ▸ **Don't be a hobby.** Show income for three out of the last five years for your holding LLC. If you fail to do so, the IRS may qualify you as a hobby and you could lose your business deductions.

- ▸ **Don't stretch it.** There are plenty of aggressive tax-deduction techniques. Be aggressive, but only so much. Take one step at a time, and consult with a great CPA who gets real estate—not many do or care to. One such technique I was considering is cost segregation. This allows you to depreciate a property much faster than straight line depreciation, which depreciates the property over 27.5 years. However, I abandoned this idea despite initial excitement. The benefit would be massive, but I've parked it for a while. Another one is claiming real estate professional status, which would allow you to write off any passive losses from your regular income—heaven! Doable, but there are a few stringent rules that must be followed, and when managing multiple properties, it becomes complicated. This should definitely only be done under the guidance of a good and knowledgeable CPA. I've parked this idea too.

▶ **Pay for audit protection.** This is a no-brainer. When filing taxes via TurboTax or your CPA, pay extra for audit assistance upfront; this is really a no-brainer. If you happen to be selected for a tax audit by the IRS, you don't want to be the one face-to-face with them. Imagine if the IRS agent asks something and you have no clear answer for whatever reason. That could drive the audit in the wrong direction. Alternatively, when someone represents you, it's totally legitimate for your representative to say, "I need to get clarity on this with my client." I am using TurboTax MAX for the mere cost of $50, or something like that. In case I would happen to be the winner of IRS Bingo, TurboTax's CPAs would be my representatives at no extra cost. Hiring someone after being selected for an audit may require paying top dollar.

▶ **Reduce friction with online tools.** Use cloud storage to scan and file all relevant documents—LLC incorporation documents; final closing statements from property purchases; lease agreements with tenants; and other legal entity-, asset-, and tenant-related docs. I use Microsoft's OneDrive only because I use Outlook.com for my email needs. I use Intuit's QuickBooks Online to manage my business books; the benefits of this are covered in the "Bookkeeping" chapter. I use TurboTax Online Self-Employed, as I live in Washington (not DC), which is a community-property state. As such, I'm not required to file taxes as a partnership because, when the LLC is owned by both spouses, we are considered a single-member LLC, not a partnership. In other states, this may require using a different version of TurboTax and filing as a partnership. I saved on that—thank you, WA!

How-To's

HOW-TO: AVOID QUARTERLY ESTIMATED TAX PAYMENTS

To avoid quarterly estimated tax payments, follow these steps:

1. Review the latest on quarterly estimated taxes on the IRS website: https://www.irs.gov/businesses/ small-businesses-self-employed/estimated-taxes.

2. Make sure you didn't have any tax liability last year. If you did, then you will probably need to pay quarterly estimated taxes.

3. You must be a US citizen or resident alien for the whole year.

4. Your prior tax year must have covered a 12-month period.

5. If all the above are true, chances are you won't need to pay quarterly estimated taxes.

6. To avoid paying them next year, make sure you don't have any tax liability this year. To estimate the net income on which you will need to pay taxes, see "How-To: Project Year-End Net Income Using QBO and MS Excel" in the "Bookkeeping" chapter.

7. If there is a chance you will owe taxes, ask your employer (via Form W-4) to increase your tax withholdings from your day-job paycheck. This way, at year end, you will not have tax liabilities and you can avoid qualifying for estimated quarterly taxes next year.

HOW-TO: WRITE OFF YOUR PASSIVE INCOME LOSSES

To write off your passive income losses, follow one of these options:

▶ **Option 1: Earn no more than $100K annually (MAGI).** Passive income losses can be written off (up to $25K) from earned income (up to $100K). If passive income losses exceed $25K, they can be carried over to the next year and written off then. Earned income between $100K and $150K allows for a gradually reduced write-off amount, which becomes $0 at $150K (MAGI). Earning more than $150K (MAGI) eliminates the ability to write off passive losses from earned income.

▶ **Option 2: Have multiple passive income sources, such as multiple rental properties with different cash-flow levels.** Houses on bigger lots will have fewer losses due to lower depreciation, creating an opportunity for greater cash flow that can offset your passive losses on other properties. A bigger down payment will drive lower monthly liabilities due to lower loan repayments. This will result in greater cash flow, which can be offset by passive losses from the other properties. Also, invest in other people's businesses; this is considered passive income, which can be offset by the passive losses from your rental properties.

- ▸ **Option 3: Claim real estate professional status.** This is an aggressive technique I have yet to try. If all criteria are met, your passive losses can be offset entirely from any earned income. Tom Wheelwright calls it your "get out of jail free" card in his book, and, in a way, it is. However, this topic falls outside the scope of this book.

HOW-TO: DETERMINE WHETHER A BUSINESS EXPENSE IS DEDUCTIBLE

For a business expense to be deductible, three tests must be met:
- ▸ The expense must be business related.
- ▸ The expense must be ordinary.
- ▸ The expense must be necessary. This means that the expense helps you to make more money.

HOW-TO: ELECT A SOLE PROPRIETORSHIP FOR A SINGLE-MEMBER LLC

A single-member LLC is, by default, a sole proprietorship from the IRS's perspective. If no special election is made, then the IRS disregards the single-member LLC and considers it a pass-through entity from a tax perspective; meaning, the LLC's taxes are paid on Form 1040 on your individual tax return.

HOW TO: REPORT RENTAL INCOME FOR A SPOUSE-OWNED LLC IN COMMUNITY-PROPERTY STATES

- ▸ A spouse-owned LLC in a community-property state, such as Washington (not DC), is considered a single-member LLC.
- ▸ A single-member LLC is a disregarded entity from the IRS's perspective by default, so rental income is reported on Schedule E on Form 1040 of your joint return.

HOW-TO: REPORT BUSINESS INCOME FOR A SPOUSE-OWNED LLC IN COMMUNITY-PROPERTY STATES

▶ A spouse-owned LLC in a community-property state, such as Washington (not DC), is considered a single-member LLC.

▶ A single-member LLC is a disregarded entity from the IRS's perspective by default, so business income is reported on Schedule C on Form 1040 of your joint return.

HOW-TO: MAXIMIZE TRAVEL DAYS AS A BUSINESS DEDUCTION

To maximize travel days as a business deduction, follow these steps:

1. Apply the sandwich-day rule. This is where you schedule business-related activities in such a way that you can write off your entire trip, including the weekend. See the next steps.

2. Plan everything ahead of time: You'll want to schedule business activities for Friday and Monday with confirmations.

3. Thursday: Travel to your destination. This is a full business day.

4. Friday: Spend time on business-related activities, at least four hours.

5. Saturday and Sunday (the sandwich): Stay at the hotel and have fun. This is considered business related since it's needed due to Monday's planned business activity.

6. Monday: Engage in key business-related activity, at least four hours.

7. Tuesday: Travel back home. This is a full business day.

8. To ensure IRS audit protection, have evidence that business activities were planned ahead, backing up all communications and confirmations.

CHAPTER 8

Continuing Education

Overview

So, how do we learn from the mistakes of others vs. having to learn from our own? How do we reduce the risk of being bamboozled by the "experts?" How do we prepare ourselves so we can respond as opposed to getting caught unprepared and frantically reacting? My dad used to say, "Speak the language people understand." I am fluent in three languages and yet I find time and time again that it's not enough to simply share the same spoken language. It's also crucially important to have basic linguistic skills in each aspect of the Real Estate Investment Framework. Lenders speak "bankish," real estate agents speak "realtyish," entity incorporation specialists speak "legalese," and so on.

The "Concepts" subsections within each section of the Real Estate Investment Framework helps you to gain a basic understanding of these languages, normally foreign to mere mortals like me who have only just started in this business of real estate investment.

Operating a rental homes business is called passive income. But if you've gotten this far, you already know that to be successful and continuously grow your real estate business, it's anything but passive.

If we want to continue our success, we need to keep expanding our knowledge, and, in this chapter, I share my personal tips for continuing your education.

Design

The following diagram outlines the key components of a successful continuing education.

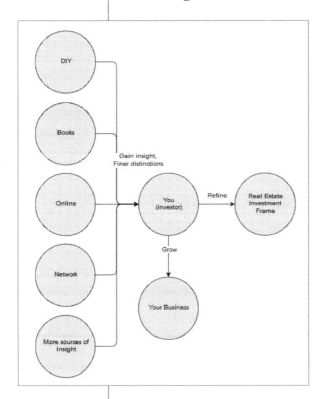

▶ **DIY.** DIY, or Do It Yourself, is when you learn something by doing it. I tried doing bookkeeping myself; I failed and hired a bookkeeper. They reconcile and balance my books periodically, although most of the transactions I categorize myself. It was the perfect education, and I learned I'd better leave it to the pros. It's turned out to be one of the most affordable investments I've made, and it has paid for itself many times over—and very quickly. Alternatively, I thought I couldn't file my taxes myself with TurboTax, so I started to shop around for a CPA who gets real estate—amazingly, not many know it well or are willing to go the extra mile and take advantage of the many tax benefits available for real estate investors. So, I reached out to a CPA who's in the know. The price of onboarding me to their services varied between $2,000 to $5,000. That's not an expense I am currently willing to do. Maybe when I have a portfolio of $100,000,000 in assets I will consider it. For my education, I turned to books, online forums, and TurboTax support, which has CPAs as a second tier. I filed my taxes in 2016 with TurboTax and it cost me less than $200, which included the TurboTax Online Self-Employed subscription and Audit Protection. That way, in case I am audited, TurboTax's CPAs will represent me vs. me having to speak to IRS agents. It took me time to figure things out by doing it myself, but now I know it and I am sharing it with you.

▸ **Books.** Books are my main source of motivation, deep knowledge, and reference, and I mostly listen to them (as audiobooks purchased on Audible). And I purchase a lot. If you were to closely look at the books I've mentioned, you'd notice a spike in the number of titles during 2015 and 2016. Why? Because I was getting ready for my real estate investment adventure—both professionally and spiritually. Audiobooks on Audible are the most expensive format on Amazon, but how ironic—they're the cheapest to "store" and deliver since they're just data. (Their expense is due to the high cost of producing them compared to a printed book.) All in all, I estimate I've spent more than $2,000 on audiobooks as of this writing. I often follow up and purchase a physical book as well. Please, don't tell my wife, Inna.

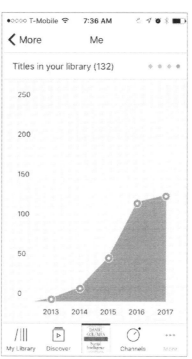

▸ **Online.** My main sources of insight and education are Facebook and BiggerPockets.com. On Facebook, I follow and befriend people who are real estate-minded. I follow what they share and ask direct questions, and they are more than happy to respond with their insights and guidance. Bigger-Pockets.com seems like Facebook for real estate investors. It's amazing how much ready-to-go content is available there. Members are insightful and quick to respond with relevant answers. There's also TurboTax. I've found a few good answers to my tax and bookkeeping questions by searching on https://community.intuit.com/quickbooks-self-employed.

▸ **Network.** It's amazing how many people I already know who've dipped their toes into real estate investing—or are aspiring to. I had no idea until I started posting my articles on LinkedIn. Suddenly, my past and current colleagues started reaching out with questions and encouragement to continue posting more articles. I met quite a few in person over lunch, and we shared insights both ways. That was very enriching.

▸ **More sources of insight.** Sources of insight are all around. When I focus on an idea, I see everything related to it. Friends, colleagues, a random chat with a stranger in line while picking up lunch or at Safeway's register. Billboards, ads, my Facebook feed, news, and other online social sites. Driving to and from work and looking around while listening to news and podcasts. I pick up bits and pieces and try connecting the dots with the focus around real estate investing.

▸ **You (investor).** This is you, who wants to get educated continuously and become more effective and efficient at growing your net worth through real estate investing.

▸ **Your business.** Your business benefits from your continuing education because you are able to avoid ineffective techniques that grow your net worth more slowly than desired—or because you're able to avoid risk in the first place. But most importantly, your continuing education results in growing your net worth faster by scaling out; that is, by constantly refining your knowledge, or, as Robert Kiyosaki would say in his book *Rich Dad's Guide to Investing*, you improve your financial intelligence by learning the finer distinctions.

▶ **Real Estate Investment Framework.** The Real Estate Investment Framework is the basis of the approach outlined in this book. That doesn't mean it cannot be refined based on what you learn and focus on. For example, I target single-family homes as my target niche. You may be targeting multi-family complexes. As a result, you will be educating yourself from a different angle, and, as such, you may refine the Real Estate Investment Framework's aspects—probably all of them. The basic framework stays the same—all aspects are still valid, such as target niche, tax strategy, bookkeeping, etc.—but the contents will need to be refined and optimized around multi-family complexes. The same with house flipping; it will bring a different set of details, yet the framework will be the same.

Strategy

The key objective of continuing education is to improve your business's growth by effectively communicating with all involved at any stage of the Real Estate Investment Framework. Failure to effectively communicate and focus on the things that matter the most will result in wasted time at best or monetary loss at worst. Being bamboozled is another risk better avoided and mitigated by being adequately prepared. By adequately prepared, I don't mean getting an attorney's license in the state where you'll be operating a rental homes business or getting a property management certification, a CPA certification, or becoming a real estate agent. Not at all. But learning the basic language for each aspect of the Real Estate Investment Framework is really helpful. To give you a head start, each chapter in this book has a "Concepts" section that gives you a primer on each aspect of the framework in down-to-earth language. Start there and it will lead to further knowledge muscle-building, providing you with additional channels outlined in the "Design" sections. You will be surprised how little each specialist you work with (CPAs, attorneys, incorporation specialists, etc.) knows about the other specialties—and often they don't know anything outside of their discipline at all. But when you meet a knowledgeable specialist that easily crosses over between the disciplines (and can offer you big-picture advice), you are faced with premium charges (albeit well deserved)! Get educated and keep more money to yourself while getting exponential results at the same time. There are times when you will want to hire a specialist, and educating yourself will allow you to hold a meaningful conversation with them in a shorter time—they usually charge by the hour—while getting clear answers to your questions. Alternatively, you may realize you need another specialist altogether, as the one you're dealing with is clueless. Here are a few things to keep in mind:

> **Challenge the pro in his backyard.** I'm a big fan of this one. Never be afraid to ask questions that may put the pro on their toes. Do it and see when they hit their limits. Are you comfortable with these limits when partnering with them? If not, you may want to hire another pro who can take you to the next level.

> **Identify authorities in the space.** List out key people, books, and online resources that specialize in each aspect of the Real Estate Investment Framework, tailored to your individual needs. You will have a head start when you review the "Resources" chapter later in this book, and many books are already listed throughout each chapter. Follow them and network proactively, as outlined in the next chapter.

> **Keep track and document.** You'll need to find a way to keep and organize the insights you collect; there will be plenty and then some. This book is my effort to organize my knowledge. On the one hand, my head was exploding with the amount of information I was exposed to and needed to preserve; on the other hand, I was losing it... I mean, yeah, I was going insane with the amount of info, but, eventually, I was forgetting it, and without any way to offload it to persistent storage, it was wiped from my working memory.

> **Never stop educating yourself.** This is paramount. Even if everything were frozen and would never change, there is so

much to learn. But things are in constant motion. The current administration is proposing a tax reform which would cap the tax rate at 15% for small businesses, while today I report on Schedule C and I am taxed at my current tax bracket, which is pretty high. Millennials are moving to the suburbs and need more single-family homes—yay! But what about the Baby Boomers? They are offloading their homes and moving to warmer and cheaper places. That may change my views on my target niche. Amazon is hiring like nuts, causing San Francisco to shake in its pants as it looks at how Seattle housing prices are going through the roof. In March 2017, Seattle was #1 nationally in home appreciation, at a stunning 26%, with Dallas a distant second at "only" 16%. This is cyclical and will change too. These are only a few examples that should give you enough motivation to never stop educating yourself, mostly through networking (either online or in person).

▸ **Send the elevator back down.** I saw this recently on either LinkedIn or Facebook, and it was attributed to Kevin Spacey, which may not be true and is irrelevant anyway. But the key message was that everyone got a ton of help on their way up, and, as payback, they need to send the elevator back down. This book is my way of sending the elevator back down to those who aspire to learn the terrain of real estate investing. I am grateful to my mentors, and I am passing on the knowledge they passed on to me via this book and my online presence via LinkedIn and Facebook. Hit me up online, and let's connect!

▸ **Start with the basics.** Learn the things that matter the most. Start with the "Concepts" sections offered in each chapter of this book.

Concepts

There's not much geek-speak in this section. There's no HOA or HELOC or other weird acronyms. If there were, that would be counterproductive for a chapter on continuing education.

Guidelines

▶ **Get educated.** Start with the "Concepts" sections within each chapter of this book, and then expand to research further online.

▶ **Network.** Build and continuously grow your network of influence and insights. To learn more, proceed to the next chapter of this book—"Networking."

CHAPTER 9

Networking

Overview

No one is self-made. Any so-called "self-made" successful person stands on the shoulders of giants—or a strong network of very smart folks. So, how do we build such a network? This chapter addresses this question. Many of the books I've read and resources I have researched often call you to build your team—in this case, a lender, real estate agent, legal specialist, CPA, bookkeeper, handyman, etc. These are all crucial. However, I'd rather build a network that is broader and less limiting. What are the sources of insight I can tap into for my burning issues or long-term challenges? Having clearly mapped out a network in each area of the Real Estate Investment Framework will help you to address both your immediate and long-term needs.

Design

Review the key components of successful networking in the following diagram:

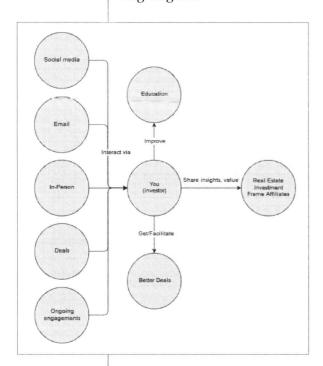

▸ **Social media.** Social media includes popular sites such as Facebook, Twitter, and LinkedIn. I am personally using Facebook and LinkedIn to reach out to like-minded people to share insights, build relationships, ask questions, and give answers. Besides these common social sites, when I need to really ask deep-dive questions that I cannot find answers to online, my go-to is the BiggerPockets.com forums, hands down.

▸ **Email.** This is my favorite way of communicating, as it doesn't require continuous, timely contact like most other mediums. This is considered asynchronous communication (as opposed to synchronous, real-time communication, like over the phone or instant messaging). Another thing I love about email is that I can effectively use it as a task manager to follow up, edit inline, store in folders, and categorize. I perfected a whole system on how to effectively write and manage email communications. This may be a topic for another book!

▸ **In-person.**

▸ **Deals.** Deals are the perfect context for making new connections. I met a good title and escrow officer during one of my deals who helped me to save close to $2,000.

▸ **Ongoing engagements.** This is after the deal is closed and you are in ongoing operational mode. Interacting with tenants and professionals who provide service to your properties (or related services), all of these are rich interactions with limitless potential to increase your network of influence and improve your knowledge.

▸ **Education.** All these networking channels offer rich interactions with a plethora of great information. Eventually, this info either needs to be processed and adopted or discarded as irrelevant. Better networking leads to better education which leads to more effective and efficient interactions. Ultimately, this leads to scoring better deals and growing your net worth faster.

▸ **You (investor).** This is you, the investor. You want to grow your network.

▸ **Better deals.** A better deal is characterized by an increase in net worth with the least effort and friction. You can only do so much yourself. To score better deals, you need to scale out through your network. And that applies to the various aspects of the Real Estate Investment Framework. The currency of exchange could be simple reciprocity—you help me with this, and I help you with that—or simply scaling out by paying for a service to shorten the time spent on a deal (so you can use that time to score another deal). In my case, bookkeeping is definitely one of the most affordable and best investments I could make, and it pays for itself in terms of the accuracy of my books.

▸ **Real Estate Investment Framework affiliates.** You build your network not only to get value from it but also to offer value back to it in equal measure. In each aspect of the Real Estate Investment Framework, you will have at least one (and often more than one) affiliate in your network. I built a network and surround myself with affiliates who are insightful and effective at what they do. Naturally, referrals are one of the most valuable currencies, which I try to pay back into the network in addition to standard fees. It's hard not to notice how I promote my bookkeeper throughout this book, right? I enjoy their services so much I feel I need to pay them back by referring them in addition to paying their fees. The same with my real estate agent and others in my network. In return, I am getting a high quality of service, insights that are so important, and, at the same time, monetary benefits as well. Pay back into your network, especially with referrals, to help your affiliates scale out their revenue streams with your help.

Strategy

The key objective of networking is to improve your effectiveness by scaling out. By effectiveness, I mean faster, friction-free growth of your net worth. Finding better, valuable, priced-under-market deals; getting financing on great terms with zero friction throughout the process (and closing on time); getting excellent, maintenance-free tenants; and streamlining your tax filing (without any unpleasant surprises by April 15th) are just a few examples of how great networking practices can contribute to your success as a real estate entrepreneur.

Concepts

There is not much to talk about here. You should be familiar with the key components to successful networking, as outlined in the "Design" section within this chapter. Networking should be natural over any channel.

Guidelines

- ▸ **Grow your network.** Be proactive in continuously growing your network of influence, whether that's online or in person.
- ▸ **Offer value first.** Offer value first and don't expect anything in return. If you realize that the other party never reciprocates, offer a gentle nudge and remind them that it would be great to have it both ways.
- ▸ **Pay back into your network.** Don't wait to be pulled in, work in push mode.
- ▸ **Broadcast value to your network without being asked for it.**

▶ **Reach out.** Don't be shy to reach out and ask for help or make the connection first. I learned that people in the vast majority of cases are willing to expand their networks as well, and your gesture is usually very much welcome.

How-To's

HOW-TO: WRITE EFFECTIVE EMAILS

To write an effective email, follow these steps:

1. Each email has to have a single objective.
2. If you need to achieve several objectives, split it into separate emails.
3. Decide what type of email it is: taking action or information sharing.
4. Decide what objective the email needs to achieve. For example:
   ▶ Convey key information (information sharing).
   ▶ Obtain clear agreement or rejection (action).
   ▶ Request materials (action).
   ▶ Establish a relationship (action).
5. The subject line must convey a key objective and should be short.
   ▶ Good: FYI – I can't make it tomorrow.
   ▶ Good: Clarity wanted on our deal.
   ▶ Bad: Remember the deal we were talking about last? I want to chat more.
   ▶ Bad: Hello.
   ▶ Bad: Question.
   ▶ Bad: <<no subject at all>>
   ▶ Bad: It's your lucky day!
6. The message body must start with a brief greeting. The follow-up chain must address the recipient by name when addressing an individual or "Dear all" (or similar) if addressing multiple recipients.

7. The first line should be a one-liner and a slightly longer version of the subject line, making sure it conveys the key message or objective. For example:

   ▸ Beg your pardon, but I can't make it to our meeting tomorrow.

   ▸ Regarding the deal on 123 Main St., please clarify the contingency on financing.

   ▸ Got your contact from <<mutual acquaintance>>, would love to connect.

8. Add a blank line after the first line.

9. Offer a few lines of supporting info.

10. Don't start with supporting info upfront. You make the recipient work harder to read your email.

11. Don't bother your recipient with your excuses. It's poison both ways.

12. Don't use jargon and TLAs (Three Letter Acronyms, or any acronyms) with someone you barely know.

13. Don't add smiley faces or other emojis; you come across as childish vs. as a business partner.

14. Don't add multiple exclamation marks; you come across as childish vs. as a business partner.

15. Don't write long emails. It indicates it will be time consuming working with you unless specifically asked.

16. Don't write long sentences. They're hard to read on mobile devices. Add line breaks often.

17. Break down multiple items into bulleted lists so the recipient can skim through easily vs. trying to parse your blurb of text multiple times before giving up.

18. Indicate future time frame specifics. For example:

   ▸ Closing is next Tuesday, time sensitive.

   ▸ I will follow up by the end of the week.

19. Add a signature that includes at least your name and preferably a way to contact you. I list a business phone number and my online presence contact details; that could be Facebook, LinkedIn, or a dedicated website.

20. Add yourself to the CC line before sending so you get the message in your inbox and experience firsthand what it's like on the other end. Use it as a follow-up technique. Now that it's in your inbox, file or tag it in the proper folder, and, when the time comes, just hit the Reply All button to circle back.

CHAPTER 10

Putting It All Together

Okay, now let's take everything we have learned so far and bring it together in a typical investment situation!

SCENARIO: Buying a Single-Family Rental with a Down Payment from Savings or from the Equity in Your Primary Residence

Scenario

Consider the following scenario:

- You have $100K to spare for investment.
- You want to purchase a cash-flowing rental property.

Solution

1. Get your credit score in shape well beforehand. See:
    - How-To: Control Your Credit Score Using CreditKarma.com

2. Identify your target niche. See:
   - ▸ How-To: Use Zillow.com to Find Target Properties
   - ▸ How-To: Use Redfin.com to Find Target Properties
3. Estimate potential cash flow. See:
   - ▸ How-To: Use Zillow.com to Quickly Estimate Cash Flow
   - ▸ How-To: Use Refin.com to Quickly Estimate Cash Flow
4. Compare estimated cash flow with the market's current rent levels. See:
   - ▸ How-To: Use Trulia.com to Quickly Evaluate the Rentals Market
   - ▸ How-To: Use Hotpads.com to Quickly Evaluate the Rentals Market
5. Research the market for loans and secure funding with your preferred lender. See:
   - ▸ How-To: Use Zillow.com to Compare Mortgage Rates
6. Work with a real estate agent to submit your offer and win the bid.
7. Market the property to target prospective renters. See:
   - ▸ How-To: Publish for Rent on Zillow.com, Trulia.com, and Hotpads.com
8. Identify qualified prospective tenants, take applications, and sign the lease. See:
   - ▸ *The Book on Rental Property Investing*. Use the forms that come with the book.
   - ▸ How-To: Conduct a Background Check of Potential Renters Using TransUnion's MySmartMove.com
9. Go over the lease agreement with the renter to clearly identify each party's responsibilities.
10. Set up a legal entity if it makes sense in your situation. See:
    - ▸ How-To: Determine If You Need to Set Up an LLC
11. Open a business bank account and business credit card.
12. Sign up for QBO and hire a bookkeeper to create the initial chart of accounts to match your rental property business.
13. Outline your tax strategy. Review the "Strategy" subsection within the "Tax Strategy" chapter. Also, see:

- ▶ How-To: Avoid Quarterly Estimated Tax Payments
- ▶ How-To: Write Off Your Passive Income Losses
- ▶ How-To: Determine Whether a Business Expense Is Deductible
- ▶ How-To: Elect a Sole Proprietorship for a Single-Member LLC
- ▶ How To: Report Rental Income for a Spouse-Owned LLC in Community-Property States
- ▶ How-To: Report Business Income for a Spouse-Owned LLC in Community-Property States

14. Keep the property in top shape. See:
    - ▶ How-To: Use Sears Home Services to Order Repairs or Maintenance

RESOURCES

My list of resources could be a book of its own! But to keep it focused and simple, below are the best of the resources mentioned in this book, as well as a few more.

CALCULATORS

- ▶ 401(k) Retirement Calculator
  http://www.bankrate.com/calculators/retirement/401-k-retirement-calculator.aspx
- ▶ Budget
  https://smartasset.com/mortgage/budget-calculator
- ▶ Cost of Living
  https://smartasset.com/mortgage/cost-of-living-calculator
- ▶ Cost of Living
  http://money.cnn.com/calculator/pf/cost-of-living/index.html
- ▶ Depreciation Calculator
  http://www.free-online-calculator-use.com/macrs-depreciation-calculator.html#calculator
- ▶ Home Rate of Return as Investment
  http://money.cnn.com/calculator/pf/home-rate-of-return/
- ▶ Inflation Calculator
  http://www.dollartimes.com/inflation/inflation.php

- ▶ Investment Property Calculator (my favorite)
  http://www.goodmortgage.com/Calculators/Investment_
  Property.html
- ▶ Net Worth and Personal Finance Management
  www.Mint.com
- ▶ Rent vs. Buy
  https://www.trulia.com/rent_vs_buy/
- ▶ Retirement Calculator
  https://smartasset.com/retirement/retirement-calculator
- ▶ Wealth Evaluator
  http://provisionwealth.com/free-resources/
  wealth-evaluator/

Books

- ▶ *Boss Life: Surviving My Own Small Business*
  Paul Downs (Blue Rider Press, 2015)
- ▶ *Deduct It!: Lower Your Small Business Taxes*
  Stephen Fishman, J.D. (NOLO, 2019)
- ▶ *Every Landlord's Tax Deduction Guide*
  Stephen Fishman, J.D. (NOLO, 2018)
- ▶ *Loopholes of Real Estate*
  Garrett Sutton (RDA Press, 2013)
- ▶ *Rich Dad Poor Dad: What the Rich Teach Their Kids About
  Money That the Poor and Middle Class Do Not!*
  Robert T. Kiyosaki (Plata Publishing, 2017)
- ▶ *Sell or Be Sold: How to Get Your Way in Business and in Life*
  Grant Cardone (Greenleaf Book Group Press, 2012)
- ▶ *Start Your Own Corporation: Why the Rich Own Their
  Own Companies and Everyone Else Works for Them*
  Garrett Sutton (RDA Press, 2012)
- ▶ *Tax-Free Wealth: How to Build Massive Wealth
  by Permanently Lowering Your Taxes*
  Tom Wheelwright (BZK Press, 2018)
- ▶ *The Book on Managing Rental Properties: A Proven System
  for Finding, Screening, and Managing Tenants with Fewer
  Headaches and Maximum Profits*
  Brandon Turner, Heather Turner (Bigger Pockets, 2015)

- *The Book on Rental Property Investing: How to Create Wealth and Passive Income Through Intelligent Buy & Hold Real Estate Investing!*
  Brandon Turner (Bigger Pockets, 2015)

- *The Millionaire Next Door: The Surprising Secrets of America's Wealthy*
  Thomas J. Stanley, William D. Danko (Taylor Trade, 2010)

- *Why "A" Students Work for "C" Students and Why "B" Students Work for the Government*
  Robert T. Kiyosaki (Plata Publishing, 2013)

Community & More

- https://www.BiggerPockets.com (#1 place to ask any question about real estate investment)

- https://www.RealWealthNetwork.com (subscribe to the podcast)

- http://www.LLCsExplained.com/

- https://www.CorporateDirect.com/resources/

ABOUT THE AUTHOR

ALIK LEVIN started his venture in real estate in 2016 by buying a condo, followed by a couple of single-family homes later that year, for the purpose of renting them out. In the years since, he has continued acquiring rental properties, now generating $220,000 annually in gross rental income.

Alik's first year was difficult in every possible way as he learned the ropes of real estate through books, online forums, advice, and firsthand experience. But as patterns emerged, running the rentals became, as they say, "business as usual"—the hunt for the properties, securing financing, signing leases, maintenance, taxes, bookkeeping, and so on. Along the journey, he relentlessly took notes, which eventually grew into the body of knowledge that shapes this book.

A particularly unique and valuable part of this experience is Alik's continuation of his full-time career as an information-technology professional while building his real estate holdings on the side. He hopes this will encourage readers not to be quick to give up their day jobs or real estate, as he proves you can truly manage both pursuits.

Alik and his wife, Inna, have three kids, who all participate in his real estate investing adventure as well. In addition, he manages a private Facebook group called *Real Estate Adventures with the Levins*.

To contact the author, inquire about large-quantity purchases,
or obtain other information related to this book, please email:
Info@OwnYourFutureForum.com

Made in the USA
Middletown, DE
08 January 2020